BY STRUTHERS BURT

THE OTHER SIDE

THEY COULD NOT SLEEP

THE DELECTABLE MOUNTAINS

WHEN I GREW UP TO MIDDLE AGE

THE DIARY OF A DUDE-WRANGLER

THE INTERPRETER'S HOUSE

CHANCE ENCOUNTERS

SONGS AND PORTRAITS

JOHN O'MAY AND OTHER STORIES

CHARLES SCRIBNER'S SONS

THE OTHER SIDE

THE OTHER SIDE

BY

STRUTHERS BURT

CHARLES SCRIBNER'S SONS

NEW YORK · LONDON

1928

Printed in the United States of America

TO MY CHARMING SISTER

ALICE

NOT WITHOUT SOME DEGREE OF AFFECTIONATE MALICIOUSNESS, SINCE SHE CHOOSES TO LIVE ENTIRELY OUTSIDE HER OWN COUNTRY

FOREWORD

FOREWORDS, as a rule, I detest, since, in nine times out of ten, they are either an apology or an admission that something that should have been said in the text has been omitted. Moreover, I have never come across any one except myself who reads them. But in a book of scattered papers such as this, written and published at various times, a foreword should both be written and read. It should be written in order to disarm any criticism that here and there the author is repetitious; it should be read, so that the intent and reasoning behind what is of its nature a loosely hung-together volume, will be doubly clear.

As to the repetition, I make no excuses; indeed, at times, in going over my proofs, I have spared repetition where I could have deleted it. I do not care so long as my meaning is sufficiently obvious. When you have something you really want to say, lucidity is the primary object. I have even reached the point where platitudes no longer bother me, so long as they are platitudes which seem to me true. Nowadays there is a great to-do about platitudes. In order to avoid them almost any loyal modernist will tell any number of lies. But meanwhile I notice that the statement of a platitude is usually received as the statement of a new and earth-shaking truth. So much, then, for the fact that these papers often repeat themselves and frequently say things that people ought to know, but don't. Where their theme is concerned, that, however, is a different question.

In a Parisian barber-shop an elderly Englishman mistook me for an Englishman, because, I dare say, I came in neither spitting, intoxicated, nor waving a little flag. Few Americans spit, not many—even in Paris—are persistently drunk, and I have seen hardly any Americans of more than five years standing who wave little flags. But, since the days of Mrs. Trollope, Dickens, and Captain Basil Hall, these marks have, in the English mind, distinguished transatlantic conduct. When they are absent, any one who speaks English must be English. That is a law as natural as that wild-fowl fly south in autumn. My elderly acquaintance, surprised that I was not an Englishman, congratulated me upon being, at all events, an American living in Paris. I informed him I was not living in Paris, but was sailing for home in a week.

"Dear me, how you must regret it!"

My patience somewhat exhausted, I replied

that, to the contrary, I was quite content, for whatever faults America might have, and these faults were numerous, and I doubted if any American was more aware of them than I, none the less, in my humble opinion, America was a vitally interesting country.

That, then, is the first object of these papers—to hint that America, whatever its faults, is a vitally interesting country. This might be called, however, a secondary object, for my words in this respect are addressed only to Americans. The European, no matter how much he may dislike us, makes no such mistake. He knows that we are interesting, if only in a horrible way. How can America be the dull, drab place that the expatriate, living somewhat drearily abroad, finds it, if so many different sorts of volumes can be written about it by so many different sorts of Frenchmen, Englishmen, Germans, Italians and Swedes?

My second and more important object is to speak to both Americans and foreigners, and for this purpose I have adopted throughout the ancient conversational methods of the pot and the kettle, not on the theory that two follies make a wisdom, but on the theory that Paul's First Epistle to the Corinthians, chapter 13, especially the 4th verse, had much to say.

I believe that on every occasion the United

States should have pointed out to it, both by foreign observers and native observers, its crimes and inconsistencies, but not under the present assumption that the United States alone is evil. Such an assumption merely defeats whatever good may be contained in criticism alien or domestic, for it arouses a natural resentment instead of a desire to learn. In addition to the First Epistle to the Corinthians, and certain verses of the Sermon on the Mount, there were, if I remember, some exceedingly philosophic words said on the subject of the throwing of stones. I would not for the world prohibit stone-throwing. There are many Goliaths of evil to be slain, but the slingers should not strut about too self-righteously. Europe is not such a pretty place if you know it well.

In short, I quite honestly believe, after most careful observation and study, that many as are the vices Americans have, they have no vice which they do not share with humanity at large, the sole difference being that this is a huge country so that everything, vice or virtue, is multiplied. This applies to the fact that, having decided within the past decade or so, and under the banner of that redoubtable warrior, Field-Marshal Mencken, to criticise ourselves, there is nowhere nowadays such an army of self-critics as in America. They march in battalions, regiments, and divisions. At the moment it is considered in American intellectual circles the height of bad taste to speak the slightest praise of one's own country—even when deserved. And if a fellow citizen raises his voice in the mildest sort of protest he is trampled underfoot. Between the Ku Klux Klan on the one side and *The American Mercury* on the other, temperate thought is difficult. All of which, as I attempt to point out in a paper called "No Gentlemen Present," increases the difficulty of the foreign observer. No alien can quite understand the American passion for completion. No alien can quite understand the groanings and flingings-about of the American radical; his ruthlessness. The French radical always admits that there are a few good people besides himself in France, and that about France there is after all something lovable, but the American radical is convinced that there is not a single fellow countryman who possesses the slightest knowledge of political or social salvation, and that his country is lost, damned and betrayed. So much for the Puritan turned prophet. John Bunyan would have understood him.

This mass criticism, it seems to me, has been, and still is, despite the fact that its present objects are almost accomplished, an excellent thing, and I wish to emphasize the fact that I approve of it and have frequently been part of it, and intend whenever occasion arises, to be part of it again. I regard Mr. Mencken as one of the most expert plumbers the world has ever seen, and value him as such. An honest, forthright, fighting plumber; well educated but singularly unripe. A crackling, strident voice such as his was sorely needed, and this myopic prophet has done an immense amount of good —also harm. As for Sinclair Lewis, no brighter or more promising plumber's assistant has yet been found. A country up-bringing and a sturdy, naïve point of view brings to his work a perpetual vigor. All either of these expert mechanics has to do is to enter a house, to discover at once where the drainage is dislocated. But drainage is not all of life, nor is it the whole truth, although I admit that nothing can go right if it is wrong. This problem of drainage has been pretty well attended to, anyway, in the decade since the war and is still in capable hands, and so it seems to me time to take stock of what has been done and to attempt some sort of estimate. You can't go on tearing up pipes forever. Sooner or later somebody will want to use the bathroom.

I am not, therefore, a conservative, and do not wish to be taken as such. I am not in love with the status quo, and mostly despise it. But I think the time has come when the attack upon the status quo should be made more gently and subtly, and a few of its pleasant features noted as well as its obviously bad ones. A trace of humanity is not out of place even in satire.

If I could sum up my general philosophy in a few words, I would say that it rests upon a passionate belief in aristocracy—in its real sense; the recognition and power granted to the best—but that this belief is dependent upon an equally passionate conviction that aristocracy can only be achieved through the slow and stumbling process of democracy, otherwise you will have no such thing as trained and responsible aristocrats. To be spiritually an aristocrat, a man must begin by being spiritually a democrat. That is no paradox, but a simple philosophical truth. I do not believe in Mr. Mencken's superman or in political panaceas. Aristocracy can be achieved only through education and economic processes.

When you take stock of all that has happened in the United States during the last ten years you find several fairly salient truths. This deluge of self-criticism is not an alarming phenomenon, it does not mean that America has suddenly become rotten, but merely that certain changes have occurred in the national life. Until the year 1900 most of the vigor and intelligence of America went into material expansion, where, at the time, it should have gone; since 1900, much of this vigor and intelligence, opportunity having been greatly restricted and the country fairly well settled up, has gone into the things of the mind. The young engineer of the eighties has become the young critic of to-day. He is a very vigorous fellow and, like most pioneers, has very little patience with those who have gone before him. If you wish to discover a rabid anti-materialist hunt for the son of a bank president. Therefore, this flood of self-criticism, far from being a sign of national decay, is a sign of national virtue, and a proof that nowadays there are more Americans thinking idealistically, and more vigorous Americans thinking idealistically, than ever before.

But if all this is excellent in the home-circle, it is not so excellent at large, as I try to point out several times in the pages which follow. There is a maturer point of view, and when dealing with foreign critics this maturer point of view is essential, if for no other reason than to save these foreign critics from themselves. One must say to these foreign critics, look here, don't swallow this whole. What we are doing is good for us, but very bad for you if you consider it a complete picture of America. It is more than bad, it is positively dangerous. As time goes on there will be built up the idea of a country so monstrous that the object of all sensible men will be to destroy it as speedily as possible. Some other Peter the Hermit will preach a crusade.

It is the thought of the horror, the inanity, the dreadfulness of this crusade, even if it culminates in no more than a social, spiritual, and critical crusade, that impels me to write as I do. I do not see how anybody could have lived through the last war without desiring for the world, with a consuming passion, better appreciation of international problems, more good nature, more tolerance, some degree of mutual laughter. There is no reason any sane man can conceive why Englishmen, Americans, Frenchmen, Roumanians, Italians, Serbs, should hate each other. No reason at all. I agree with H. M. Tomlinson; the mere mention of war makes me physically ill. I cannot read the dry-as-dust little treatises of those who study war without my foot itching for a kick. "The opening of war would send the civil population gibbering to its cellars with demolition bombs. This would be followed by an assault with gas-bombs which would send heavier-than-air gas seeping down into every crevice, killing the population like rats in their holes. . . . The more savage, bitter, and rapid the aerial combat, the quicker could the final decision of battle be reached."

I suppose as long as the world is in its present mood such statements, and the studies back of them, are necessary, but the man who does not qualify them by a personal hatred of war, be he general or air-cadet, is as dangerous as an escaped lunatic. If, however, you want such conditions as these, continue to permit without temperate discussion, the growing European delusion in regard to us and continue to permit without insisting upon the reverse of the shield, the present drastic native criticism. Do not try to suppress either of them, that is invariably dangerous, even were it not, where the latter is concerned, stupid. Be a critic yourself. In criticism lies growth. But when you have said your say on that side, say it, for the love of peace, on the other. Men are slow to quarrel with those who seem to them human and much like themselves.

And so the second salient truth which emerges from a casual stock-taking, seems to me to be the necessity for all thinking Americans, first, to try to understand America as best they can, and after that, to try to explain America, as best they can, to the rest of the world. I put this once more upon the most practical and urgent foundations. It is tiresome to take an interest in politics, it is tiresome to regard social conditions, even more tiresome to discuss such questions seriously; but the most tiresome thing of all would be to have your wife "gibbering in a cellar," and your son engaged in an aerial combat where savagry, bitterness, and rapidity are the factors of success. We are living in a changed world, thinking has become necessary. Without it a man can no longer survive. But it is not thinking alone that will save him. He must think quickly as well. Yet even that is not enough. He must think, he must think quickly, and then, when he has done all that, he must think wisely. If this is necessary at street corners, how much more necessary is it in national and international affairs.

Finally, lest there be too much misunderstanding, although, no matter what I say, there will be some misunderstanding, for it is impossible so to write or speak that certain people will not misunderstand you, let me state, as I state repeatedly in the subsequent pages, that I like all nations, and especially those who speak my own tongue. Indeed, I believe, with unshakable conviction, that as things now are, the one hope of the world, politically, lies in more toleration between the English-speaking peoples. Later on I explain why toleration is the ideal. Understanding is too much to expect. But this is a frank age and a fairly grim one, and the most futile approach to any clarity of vision is an approach about which clings the slightest hint of sentimentality. "Hands across the sea" is an antedated slogan. It is regarded, and justly, with suspicion. As an American I have certain grievances.

Let me state them, right or wrong. I do so without malice and without hatred. Where I am wrong I am willing to be corrected, where the other man is wrong let him take steps to correct himself. So, too, the Englishman and Frenchman have numerous grievances. Let them state these grievances, nor mince words in so doing. I, for one, will be glad to hear them. I do not believe in suppression, and, although frankness may create a temporary misunderstanding, in the end and cumulatively it is the only agent that produces any sort of permanent good-will.

Nothing I say is either provocative or inflammatory, and if any reader of this volume lays it down with the statement that, for example, I hate England, I wish to tell him now that he is either a liar, a fool, or of invidious intention, whether he be an American or a European. I like England, indeed I love her, far better than those who believe that you can cure a danger by denying it, just as I love my own country far too well to listen with patience to the statements of the average American.

Hibernia,
Southern Pines, North Carolina,
December 1, 1927.

CONTENTS

I

THE SENSE OF LAW

I

THE SENSE OF LAW

ON that far-off and perfect day when human affairs are managed properly, someone will write a book showing the reverse side of specialism, and one of the first sanctuaries to be turned inside out in this fashion will be the one which states that "fools rush in where angels fear to tread." They do, and the air is nervous with the winds of their rushing, but one forgets that more than half the time the angels are responsible and that, much as the fools fumble and confuse matters, where other bodies are concerned their meddling is inevitable and necessary. Fools, after all, are frequently no more than laymen, amateurs, that is to say—the ignorant, the victims, the public—while angels are experts, and nothing is more certain than that experts are constantly in need of the opinion, sometimes even of the [illegible].

In his essay on the jury system Chesterton has shown now that apparently cumbersome and old-styled method of determining guilt is not only the

I

THE SENSE OF LAW

ON that far-off and perfect day when human values are reassessed properly, some one will write a book showing the reverse side of aphorisms, and one of the first aphorisms to be turned inside out in this fashion will be the one which states that "fools rush in where angels fear to tread." They do, and the air is nervous with the winds of their rushing, but one forgets that more than half the time the angels are responsible and that, much as the fools hamper and confuse certain issues, where other issues are concerned their rushing is inevitable and necessary. Fools, after all, are frequently no more than laymen, amateurs, that is to say—the audience, the victims, the public—while angels are experts, and nothing is more certain than that experts are constantly in need of lay opinion, sometimes even of lay revolution.

In his essay on the jury system Chesterton has shown how that apparently cumbersome and often stupid method of determining guilt is not only the symbol of a racial sense of fairness, but essential as well to the continuance of that fairness. The consensus of opinion of twelve good men and true may often be wrong-headed, but it is always human, and although one would prefer opinion to be both clear-headed and human, if it cannot be both it had better, at least in matters of life and death, be the latter. The present partly sophisticated age is cherishing, to the contrary, a belief, growing rapidly into a superstition, that what the world needs is more expert advice and less unthinking compassion. That is only a half-truth, no better than the half-truths it seeks to eliminate. The world does need more expert advice, but the expert, on the other hand, needs more lay opinion. In short, what really is needed is intelligent compassion and compassionate intelligence. Nothing is more terrible than a meeting of experts, save, possibly, a meeting of fools.

Angels know more about heaven than fools—they ought to, they live there—but the trouble is that, seeing mostly only other angels, they talk an angelic patter of their own and, what between this and that, come eventually to have a great contempt for their constituents, or clients, or patients, or public, or what you will. Not only a contempt but also a conviction that celestial details are the only things that matter. They completely forget that heaven's sole and original purpose was to afford a final abiding-place for fools, and that the stuff of which their jobs are made is the stuff of human folly. If there weren't fools there wouldn't be angels, although, if there weren't angels there would most certainly still be fools. If the fool waited at heaven's gate while the expert angel —expert, or minor official—put on swank and hemmed and hawed over tickets and raised supercilious angelic eyebrows, he would never get in at all.

For example, one does not like, even in a humble way, to encourage ignorance and prejudice and violent wrong thinking, and the common sense of the theory of evolution, also its spiritual beauty, need not be discussed; but the biologists should be reminded that if they hadn't insisted upon playing angel there would have been considerably less opportunity for the rushing in of fools—real fools this time.

Once the biologists descended from the lofty and hidden heights of experiment and step-by-step reasoning and, entering the dark valley of theology, leaped a stream in the shadows and attempted to formulate a religion, they ceased to be scientists and became poets and preachers; and, since poetry and preaching are very human affairs, the fools rushed in—two kinds of fools: the fools who find evolution profane and the fools who vaguely and mistily really do think we are descended from monkeys. Meanwhile, the biologists have not yet admitted that no science can build a religion and that no religion is unassailable, whether it be materialism or transcendentalism. Mystery remains, and God, if there be one, must regard with equal sardonicism the fundamentalist and the adherent of salt and water.

But what the scientist does, or the artist, immensely important as it is in the long run, is by no means as pressingly important as what is done by those three curious professions, or arts—there is always a discussion there—that touch continuously and immediately human nature: the professions or arts of medicine, theology, and the law, and under the last, its subsidiary branches, the lawmakers and, in the widest sense, the police. You have time to consider the biologist and reject or assimilate his teaching, but when you are sick you want a good doctor, when you are troubled about your soul, a good clergyman, and, when the body politic is ill, good lawyers, good judges, good policemen, and, above all, sensible framers of law; and you want all these without delay. The cure cannot be put off; it is a question, one way or another, of life and death. No wonder fools have to rush in, and no wonder that at present, especially in America, lay opinion where one of these fundamental professions, or arts is concerned, is steadily rising to a crisis in its bitter contempt.

The doctors are wise men; they have to be; their wares are too much in the open. Even the clergy have set about to some extent the cleaning of their house, but, blindly and blithely and insolently, the bar and the legislators and the police continue increasingly to place themselves amongst the greatest criminals of a somewhat distracted era.

I say criminals and I use the word advisedly.

Now law is a curious thing, for, although it is exceedingly susceptible to chicanery and complexity, in its essence it is exceedingly simple and homespun. You can fool the average man for a while on most questions, but on this question you cannot fool him for long, for the average man, especially the man born under the Anglo-Saxon tradition, has, ingrained in him deeper than any other feeling, save the feelings of sex and self-preservation, the sense of law. Therefore, upon no other question has the fool, or layman, more right to utter an opinion; and to outrage and thwart this sense of law is one of the most dangerous pursuits possible, even in such a sprawled and slow-moving democracy as America, even if this sense of law is usually undefined and, for a while, timidly subservient.

You not only cannot fool the average man about the law, you cannot even tell him much about it intrinsically, once he sits down to think it over. You can confuse him with legal language, you can get the better of him by trickery, you can hand him hundreds of volumes of precedent; but what the law actually is he knows because, unless he is born an idiot, he realizes that he was born into a world of law, dies according to law, and that, every night and every day, he watches things that move by law, among them the sun, the clouds, the stars. And this was true even in the days when man thought nature was the whim of the gods. The basic idea of cause and effect is the same, whether you believe rain comes from certain natural laws or because you have pleased a deity.

Law is man's admission that if you hurt another man you have to do something about it, even if the reaction is no more than running away; it is man's perception of three dimensions; that is, that objects possess length, breadth, and thickness, and that you cannot walk through them. It is his discovery that there are other people in the world besides himself. That is all it is, save the further discovery that some people are weak and others strong; the discovery, in other words, of the rights of the majority and the rights of the minority. You can hide theology under a veil of special and divine knowledge, you can hide medicine beneath admitted special training, but you cannot hide the basic principle of law.

Strange that all through history lawyers and judges and policemen and statesmen have had to be reminded by "fools" of such an obvious truth.

Law, therefore, is man's sense of fair play and his agreement to live with other men peaceably, conditioned, of course, by the innate perversity of circumstances and human nature. It is the most intimate thing man possesses, save, as said before, his instinct for sex and for self-preservation, and, as a matter of fact, it is a corollary of the latter, for it is an acknowledgment that the best way to preserve yourself is to preserve good sense and justice in your manners and habits and decrees where others are concerned. Law was invented, or rather it evolved itself, in the minds of ordinary people; it is a common thing, an ordinary thing, a daily thing; it is not even preserved for Sundays or illnesses, and it was only because we—the ordinary people, the fools—did not have the time, going about our usual occupations, to keep track of this discovery that it was ever turned over to trustees. When these trustees forget that they are trustees and regard themselves as inventors, then it is time to remind them of their honorable but by no means lofty position.

Furthermore, since the law is such an elemental business, you can no more fabricate it than you can make a baby. There are plenty of synthetic laws, but they bear no relation to the real thing. A real law is at hand when needed, never before and seldom long afterward, and all the pronunciamentos possible to the folly of the human mind cannot make a so-called law the law unless it is the law to begin with. There is nothing that so exposes the blocked intelligence as the statement that such and such a thing "is the law and so must be obeyed." To the lay mind, which conceived law and which must live by law, a law is not a law if it offends the sense of law, and millions of misguided experts cannot prove otherwise. The sense of law stands above all law and all laws are subject to it and refer back to it.

The English common law represents the slow evolvement of the ordinary man's desire to be at peace, as said before; not only that, but pleasantly at peace as well. Sir Edward Coke says: "Reason is the life of the law; nay, the common law itself is nothing but reason." But so is all law, even statutory law, and when, as is so often the case, statutory law is passed without any sense of law—without reason as its life—it is bound for death, as is all law that is not law.

So far so good, but to such an argument supporters of all laws as such answer of course: "Quite so, but suppose every man felt himself at liberty to pick what laws he should obey and what laws he shouldn't? Where would we be then? There are a number of people who feel that they have the right to commit murder and a still larger number of men and women who feel that the marriage laws can be twisted according to their own fancies. Even there, however, your sense of law, although perverted, is present; self-justification is the commonest of human traits."

It is—self-justification, that is—but, save in the case of abnormal people, it is born after an event, or immediately before, and is not there in the beginning, as is the sense of law. It is doubtful if the majority even of those who commit murder or abuse their wives, or husbands, once they get through with their self-justifications, mostly personal, will uphold murder or cruelty as a theory. The free-loverists, for all their noise, have always been in a small minority, perhaps not in actual practice but in their philosophy at least. Man's sense of law is involved when he involves himself with a woman, and, no matter how much he may flout this sense of law, he does not delude himself into the belief that he is practising perfect justice. The whole question, of course, comes down to one of the majority and the minority, of the normal and abnormal, and although this would seem a topic too ancient and too well known to discuss, unfortunately it has become in America the most pressing of questions. We seem to be losing our sense of the rights of the minority; that is, a large element among us seems to be losing this sense, and in this element are most legislators, most administrators of the law, and not a few judges and lawyers.

Perfect balance, of course, would be where each man could do exactly what he wanted provided he did not interfere with the rights or comfort of any one else, but since this is impossible, the rights of the minority increase in direct proportion to their numbers and their approach to what is considered normal; their approach, in other words, to the average man's sense of law. The witty French statement that insanity is merely a question of being in the minority is quite true, but we need not think about that for a while, not anyway until modern conditions—as they very well may do—accelerate even more than at present the production of a moron population. What we should think about is that the rights of the majority have never been, and never will be, the imposing of the majority's implicit will upon the minority; it has always been a sixty-forty proceeding. There is no other way of doing it, otherwise you so offend the sense of law of numerous people that sooner or later you have trouble on your hands. There is no other way, that is, save by persecution or war, and even then you are only temporarily successful.

Force majeure has been tried again and again in the world and has always failed. You can massacre or exile your opponents, but you cannot massacre or exile the idea that made them oppose you.

Louis the Fourteenth was a rationalistic monarch, so when he considered the Huguenots sufficiently dangerous he drove them out. He realized that statutory laws aimed at a man's conscience would not do, for the simple reason that such laws are not laws and cannot be made such. The Spanish kings followed the same logical method, but in the end both they and Louis the Magnificent failed. Protestantism is not dead in France, and France was greatly hurt by the expulsion of the Huguenots; Spain killed herself for all time by the Inquisition and her treatment of the Moors and the dissenters.

The sense of law, therefore, is elemental, the sense of law is perpetual, and the sense of law, more than anything else, is based upon the rights of the weaker, or the minority. But more than this, it is so much an entity that, although it cannot be utterly killed, it can be wounded and grievously sinned against.

It can be sinned against by affronting its perception of common sense as well as affronting its perception of fair play. It knows that in all things there are degrees of right and wrong.

Statutory laws may at times be necessary, although always dangerous, but to say because the sense of law has called forth one statutory law the door is open to every form of statutory law is to perform a feat of reasoning called, if I am not mistaken, chop logic. It is to say that because one egg is good for you at breakfast, twelve eggs must be twelve times better; it is also to say because in Occidental countries actual polygamy is forbidden that the spiritual and celestial marriages of the Mormon church should be forbidden also. Narcotics, for instance, are clearly and dramatically unsocial and every one knows it, but to say that because there is a law against narcotics there should be one against chocolate sundaes, although perfectly logical, is, none the less, perfectly insane. We forget too much the *reductio ad absurdum;* we forget that most over-earnest logicians, at least those who insist upon practising their logic, are locked up in institutions.

Chocolate sundaes do undoubtedly in many instances cause slow death, and there is no question that indigestion is an antisocial disease producing immense loss and misery, but since the victims of chocolate sundaes are not immediately vicious and the process of their decay spreads itself delicately over a long period, the question enters that vague field of compromise, where, until recently, humanity has agreed to mind its own business. You are at liberty to eat all the chocolate sundaes you want until you begin to throw glasses at the soda clerk's head and then, quite properly, you are arrested. The sense of law has always recognized this distinction. There were, for instance, laws against drunkenness; there were not, before war with its false legal values blurred the sense of all civilian law, laws against drinking, for drinking is not in itself antisocial; to the contrary, it may frequently be social. As a matter of fact, the act itself is neither social nor antisocial, but is in a realm outside the law, like brushing your teeth, going to bed, or taking your daily dozen.

Since the sense of law is an entity and can be sinned against, those who sin against it must be criminals in the same way as all men who sin against law, although unfortunately this has not yet been recognized formally. To pass or to promote the passage of a bad law is as criminal an act as to break a good law, to permit without protest a bad law is as foolish and as conducive to crime as to permit without protest murder, highway robbery, or arson. Worse, for whereas the latter three are obviously antisocial, the two former, although equally antisocial, go so deeply to the foundations of living, and are so hidden that they may undermine the state if allowed to proceed. From a purely moral standpoint, where bad laws are concerned, unless they can be repealed, nullification is the only attitude consistent with integrity, also with common sense.

We are witnessing to-day, more obviously in America than elsewhere, but none the less throughout the world, the curious spectacle of the law being punished by the sense of law, and this punishment will continue, with all its disastrous consequences, until the law reforms itself—the law and its administration. Authority stands responsible before the bar of real justice; and it is more guilty than recognized criminality, for it is supposed to be less hampered and better informed. Through slow centuries of warfare and revolution monarchy has at last learned what the sense of law implanted in the minds of even its humblest citizens is, and to-day the few remaining constitutional monarchies—England, Holland, the Scandinavian countries—are the only partially law-respecting countries in the world; the only countries, that is to say, where authority considers itself responsible to the people and the people consider themselves responsible to authority. Indeed, some of the Scandinavian governments have evolved even to the point where they realize that one of the functions of government is to promote such little considered necessities as the desire for gayety, the love of beauty, and the rational happiness of their citizens. A bizarre idea when one considers the present sullen dislike of most governments for their peoples and of most peoples for their governments. It is rumored that in certain Scandinavian countries officialdom even goes to the length of insisting that minor servants and the police be courteous to the ordinary man, let alone being just.

Democracies, drunk with the lawlessness of majorities, have yet to learn their lesson.

And, indeed, this insistence upon the necessity for courtesy is not fine drawn but lies at the very root of the sense of law, besides being infinitely wise on the part of officials. As law represents not only man's desire to live at peace but to live at peace pleasantly, the insolent customs official, the brutal policeman, the hectoring judge, the insulting cross-examiner, the "bawling-out" traffic officer, the impertinent fanatic, the democrat who so little understands democracy that he thinks it an opportunity for universal hoggishness, the hypocritical lawmakers, all these in their minor ways are as serious offenders against the law as the thief, the murderer, the forger, and the framers and supporters of vicious legislation. What is authority—the rich, the governments—doing to prove to those born below a certain economic level that they should be kind toward those born above? The percentage of goodness that exists under modern conditions, small as it may be, is a tribute to the inherent decency of the human race. Some day governments will learn to present themselves to their citizens as something else than a lowering menace, legal or financial; a constant insolent rebuke. If the commissions now investigating crime will indict criminal authority as well as the admitted criminal, they will do a lasting service.

But even if they don't, the world—the fools—will not forever continue to watch the liar frame laws for the comparatively honest man, the authorized thug beat the unauthorized thug, the mental prostitute sentence the far less guilty and unfortunate bodily prostitute.

The sense of law, which is man's notion that there can be pretty nearly an honest, approximately gay, and largely constructive world, has survived many vicissitudes; it will survive even the early, perhaps necessary, experiments of democracy. It not only will survive, it must, for it is the essential idea that separates man from the rest of creation; the clear break between him and the beast. It is, furthermore, the keystone of the democratic ideal. If it cracks, the arch falls.

It is a holy idea and a beautiful one.

II

THE EUROPEAN COMPLEX

II

THE EUROPEAN COMPLEX

HE said—he was talking to a lady only a few feet away and I could not help but overhear him: "Leprechauns? Certainly I believe in leprechauns. I never happen to have seen one meself, but lots of my friends have." And then, a couple of minutes afterward, he said: "Of course, ye're the most childish people in the world and we Europeans are simply amazed at you." Although he added, as they all did a year or two ago, and as a few lonely liberals still do: "But you are, none the less, the one hope of the world."

And so there you are. I cannot imagine a more accurate description of the European mind and the European attitude toward us than is contained in this ready-made parable, nor a better example of international logic. How can we be the one hope of the world if we are so childish, unless a little child shall lead them?—a refined simplicity in which no European believes.

But this is not the point; or rather, it is not the

main discrepancy. To understand the main discrepancy you must understand that all Europeans believe in leprechauns, whether it be, to pick a few instances of many, the English belief in the caricature of Uncle Sam, the French belief in the perfection of France, or the German belief in the mysterious Teutonic overman. Every European is born into a world of class stratification and presupposition, and no matter how intelligent or cultivated or clever he is, beyond a certain point he believes in fairies, and of all these fairies the international ones are the most powerful and the most malignant. Also, still further to understand the main discrepancy, you must understand that although the European believes in leprechauns, and is proud of his belief, he will allow no one else an equal privilege. Whatever the American or Canadian or Australian thinks or does is *ipso facto* immature; whatever the European does is *ipso facto* adult. And this will continue even when America and Canada and Australia are a thousand years old.

If an American believes in Bryanism, it is a sign of youth; if an Irishman believes in leprechauns, as my hero did, it is a sign of age. Mussolini in Italy is splendid, or, at least, dignified, the Ku Klux Klan in America is absurd; but no one seems to stop long enough to reflect that the only reason why, in America, the Ku Klux Klan is absurd is because, childish as America may be, it is at least sufficiently adolescent not to need the infantile cures of castor oil and unrestrained force. No wonder it is impossible for the American or the Canadian or the Australian ever to make himself clear to his various cousins. He is caught on the horns of a dilemma; he is predestined; he is damned if he will and damned if he won't.

The English boy is told at Eton or Harrow, or where you will, that Americans and Canadians and Australians are creatures of a certain kind, and he never gets over it. No European ever accepts a wise and pleasant American as partially representative of his race. A wise and pleasant American is always accepted as a sport, a freak, a survival of something European or a development toward something European. I, for instance, being an American, can tell at a glance an English gentleman from an Englishman who is not a gentleman, or a French gentleman from a bargee, or, usually, a German gentleman from a *Kellner;* but I have never yet met an Englishman or a Frenchman or a German who could reverse the process. Indeed, to make another international generalization—and I am going to indulge in a good many—I should say that one of the distinguishing marks between a European and an inhabitant of the western continents is that, although both are taught to believe in fairies, occasionally some Westerner grows up.

Within the circle of his limitations, there is no end to what a European may imagine, predict, or understand; but, internationally, that circle is bounded by Asia to the east, the Mediterranean to the south, Archangel to the north, and Dingle Bay to the west. And if this seems preposterous, I call your attention to the latest utterances of those brilliant English minds, Gilbert Chesterton, Israel Zangwill—now dead—John Galsworthy, Aldous Huxley, St. John Ervine, and so on. For example, not long ago there was a most popular book, although I hesitate to place its author in juxtaposition to the above list, for he clearly is not brilliant; in which apparently it was only necessary to say that a thing was American to condemn it, or to say that a thing was un-American to praise it. We have become, in other words, a derogatory adjective.

I have known Englishmen who have lived in America twenty years and who are American citizens, who still have as egregious ideas concerning their adopted land as if they had never left the Scilly Isles behind.

But all this is relatively unimportant. No American can make understandable either himself or his country to the European mind, and every day more Americans are beginning to realize this lamentable fact and to cease trying. When they all cease trying much time will be saved. The latest attempt *en masse*, and probably the last, was the Great War. We all know how successful that was. The future hope of the world lies not in mutual understanding, that lost ideal of a decade ago, for that is impossible, but in mutual respect and toleration. When the European regards the American, the Canadian, the Australian, and the New Zealander as aliens but equals, as the best Europeans to-day regard, let us say, the best Mohammedans, all will be well.

This paper is addressed not to the European, for to convince the European of its context would be like trying to salt the tail of the wariest bird; to the contrary, it is addressed to a large class of Americans.

Not the expatriated Americans. They, too, are hopeless. Lurking in a myriad *pensions* or castellated, to suggest a subtle pun, as the richer are, they are beyond discussion. But within the confines of America, except when they pour eastward during the summer, are thousands of fairly amenable Americans who might be prevailed upon to take a more rational point of view. It is very necessary that they should take this more rational point of view, for until they do, every steamer sailing for Europe will continue to be a focal point for the spreading of international disease.

It is very necessary that they should take a more rational point of view, for, with the possible exception of England, there is no country that contains among its intelligent classes more persistent criticism of itself and, as is not the case with England, greater misunderstanding of itself than America. The Englishman criticises his own country persistently, but he is also well aware of the virtues of his breed—perhaps too well aware; the American is all too likely to criticise America with no sense of the universal dullness of mankind.

It is easy to see why the latter is true, and hence my choice of a title. Europe is the mother of practically all of us. As history is counted, we have not been so very long away from her breasts. We are still caught in a nexus of maternal glamour; but if we are in any way immature as compared to this mother of ours, the immaturity has its source in this idea that necessarily she is more mature. We cannot grow up until the nexus is unraveled.

Self-criticism is excellent, and it is perhaps the main reason why, intellectually, neither England nor America have stopped growing, and why Germany is beginning to grow again. But it must be rational self-criticism. The attitude of the publican is a beautiful and touching and wise one, but it is not altogether wise, nor is the publican altogether a sensible fellow, until he sees out of the corner of his eye that the pharisee is an equal sinner.

Maturity is a quiet appreciation of your own faults and virtues, and a quiet but equal appreciation of the faults and virtues of your neighbor.

I do not mention the boastful American, and for this, no doubt, will earn the smiles of many foreign readers; but, to begin with, the boastful American is outside the argument, which is addressed to the apologetic American; and in the second place, the boastful American is to a great extent another European leprechaun. If he ever existed in any great quantities, he is rapidly disappearing. For one boastful American I have met in many years of traveling about Europe I have met a hundred apologetic ones. I think Mr. Tarkington's "Plutocrat" a charming book, but essentially a work of fiction. Nor are the boastful Americans, when come across by a European, always understood. There is a certain type of boasting that is the result of an exaggerated humility; there is another type of boasting that comes from a just anger.

The Englishman says to the Frenchman or American, "You have a filthy country filled with filthy people," and so on, and so on, for the English adjectives are nothing if not final; and when, at the end of half an hour or so, the Frenchman or American mildly objects, stating what he thinks are a few facts in rebuttal, the Englishman goes away convinced that he has met another flag-waving Gaul or another braggart Yankee. If he is a very nice and broad-minded Englishman, he merely raises his eyebrows and smiles and says: "How extraordinarily sensitive you people are!" But let some one try the same thing with him. Furthermore, the boastful American is usually an American of not more than twenty years' standing; and finally, he is no more boastful than any other half-idiotic national—simply more numerous.

We come back again, then, to the apologetic American and a more rational point of view.

What is this more rational point of view? Simply this: That there is nothing altogether perfect and nothing altogether imperfect, that distance not only lends enchantment but frequently induces a sort of romantic insanity; and that a common trait of the human mind is to magnify a spot on the drawing-room carpet and overlook a puddle in the highroad.

How many men are married to beautiful women with not the slightest appreciation of their good fortune? The sensible attitude, of course, is to look at both spot and puddle and so arrange your vision that every now and then you obtain a perspective upon your wife. As for me, I would take the very starkest premises, I would begin at the beginning, I would lay my cards on the table. What the world needs even more than an honest and sensible Geneva Conference, which at present it hasn't got, is a conference in humility, a pooling of its common moronism.

When all nations admit their faults and insist that these faults be recognized, then, for the first time, it will be possible really to admire their virtues.

I will begin at the beginning.

I will admit without hesitation or reservation that we are a young, crude, barbaric, folly-ridden, uncomfortable people. I will admit that we are of mongrel breed; that we have a mania for speed, size, mass, and money; and that the thoughtful, gentle, and intelligent are in the proportion of about ten to every thousand. I will admit that we are grasping, imperialistic, selfish, bombastic, and swept by passion and sentimentality. I will admit anything derogatory that any one has to say, and having admitted all this, what have I done? Why, I have described America and every other country in the world.

Let us examine this statement. Roughly speaking, a man can be judged by three factors—what he thinks, what he does, and what, outside of his thinking and doing, he is; what he was born—in other words, what he looks like. Let us take this last and possibly least important factor first.

One of the commonest charges hurled at our heads by Europeans and certain Americans, and the cause, so they believe, of many of our sins is that we are a mongrel nation. Are we?—that is, always bearing in mind that the comparison is simply with other nations. Laying aside the facts that the charge may be a compliment as far as we know, and that the last census of the United States showed a vast preponderance of Celtic and Teutonic blood, a preponderance even of blood from the British Isles—laying aside these facts as irrelevant to the present discussion, are we actually a mongrel nation as compared to any other great nation?

We are not. We are mongrel as compared to the Eskimo, but not as compared to the Frenchman, the German, the Italian, or even the Englishman. We are not mongrel enough.

Standardization with us has gone about as far as it should. We should begin to fear not diversity but homogeneity. In the last war the American Army was the only cohesive army there was, and this despite the German-speaking regiments from the Middle West and the draft division from New York.

France is usually considered the most homogeneous of the great nations of Europe, although, as a matter of fact, England is more so. Can either claim to be anything but a mongrel nation? To any one who knows France or England, and who is in the habit of examining statements, such claims are wildly absurd. Furthermore, pure blood, so-called, has until recently been a matter of class and not of nation. Now, with the increase of facilities for communication, pure blood has become not even a matter of class but of stupidity. The working man and even the peasant are beginning to marry out of their own parishes, but the aristocrat has always married out of his own parish. I defy any one to find a greater mongrel than the average English peer, save it be the French or German noble. And of them all, royalty is the most confused.

Here is the paradox. So long as communication was difficult and expensive, the lower classes were pure-blooded, the upper classes mongrel. But the very isolation of the peasant and mechanic, although it made them in their particular locality homogeneous, produced, when all these localities were lumped together into a nation, a welter of dissimilarity ruled by people invariably mongrel. Now all are going to be mongrel together.

Nor was immigration ever lacking. Beginning, although it is a late date, with the ebb and flow of the Romans and the Barbarians, and not forgetting Attila and the Moors, and the Crusades, and a hundred other migrations large and small, one can come down to the present day and the amusing but little-known truths that France has a negro problem and a problem of undigested Italian labor. The present-day newspaper headings in France are oddly similar to ours of a decade ago.

In short, in many instances France is entering upon a stage from which we are emerging. And yet, for some reason, whenever a foreigner lands upon our shores he becomes to the European and certain Americans a frightening potential factor toward heterogeneity, while, for the same obscure reason, vast armies and all the merchants and mechanics of Christendom have been going up and down the face of Europe for centuries in a state of virtue that would be unbelievable were one not assured, by implication, that it was so.

Do the French imagine that their occupied territories, already largely Teutonic, will become any the more Gallic because of the occupation? The truth of the matter is that pure blood, save for the peasant, has always been a fable, popular only with sociologists, and has never been a claim of the aristocrat.

The apologetic American is making an historical and social blunder.

It is unbelievable that any one knowing France,

with its Basque, its Provençal, its Breton, its Norman, its Alsatian, its Burgundian, and so on indefinitely, people many of whom until recently could not speak the common language of their nation, and some of whom do not speak it even now—it is unbelievable that such a person could speak of America as hybrid and France as homogeneous. It is equally unbelievable that any one knowing Great Britain, with its Scotchman, its Saxon, its Welshman, its North and South Irishmen, its Yorkshireman, Cornishman, Jerseyman, Norfolk and Suffolk men, could do the same. But nevertheless it is done. It is onc of the most frequent absurdities you hear, and an absurdity becoming more and more popular, especially on the lips of Americans.

Not long ago I had tea at a French country club with three pure-bred Englishmen. All of them were university men, two of them wore monocles. Their names were Captain Strumpelfeck—I am not giving the exact names, but names very much like the original ones—Mr. Sforza and Mr. McComas.

Law, speech, custom, preponderance of blood, the mysterious blending of stronger or weaker races give a nation its tone; these when added to climate and environment in other respects. We are a nation in the English tradition and will never escape from that fact; but we are, I am glad to say, like every other great nation, a nation of mixed blood.

So much, then, for mongrelism. But granting that it is an international and not a national attribute, what has it done to us physically? Again, only in comparison with other like nations. To judge by observation and statistics, it has done us no great harm. We are still a blondish tall nation, becoming more so. We are not ugly when compared with the rest of the world, and we seem to be able still to compete in feats of strength and swiftness. Good food and a stimulating climate have, of course, helped. And yet, although I for one am convinced that the American nation as a whole is becoming steadily better-looking, one of the commonest complaints of the apologetic American abroad is that he or she is ashamed of the appearance—we will come to the manners later—of his or her compatriot. I imagine, however, that even the most apologetic of Americans is beginning to revive a trifle, now that the English, the Germans, and even the French are also beginning to travel in organized herds.

Of course, a sensitive person—without much discrimination—is likely to become sorrowful over the antics of compatriots in a strange country, just as a sensitive person notices the vulgarities of a cousin considerably more than the vulgarities of somebody else's cousin; but the apologetic American in the past has overlooked numerous obvious facts.

Until recently the American travelled more than any one else. There was more of him or her to be sorrowful about. Eighty per cent of all crowds are vulgar. People when travelling are at their worst. It is a rare gift to travel inconspicuously and beautifully.

Moreover, solecisms spoken in your own language or performed in a familiar way are more noticeable than when spoken in a language you do not understand or when performed with a quaint exoticism.

About a gentleman from Kansas who picks his teeth there is none of the *cachet* that surrounds a French nobleman when engaged in a similar operation, and the adenoidal drinking of soup by the English can be forgiven by all save Englishmen.

Much of this, however, is changing as the other nations take to the trail. Any one who has been in Italy with the Germans in the Spring, any one who has been on a steamer filled with French, may continue to be sorrowful, but it will be for the world in general, not for America exclusively.

I wish every one could have had two experiences that I have had. Once, while I was an undergraduate at Oxford, I saw a Lancashire regiment on the march, and another time I happened to be in Brittany when fifteen thousand English landed on a three-day excursion. The latter was like an outpouring of gnomes, the former an example, almost too vivid, of what social rigidity can produce—the grotesque, asymmetrical private, the big blond fine-looking young officer of the upper middle class. In their eagerness to produce beautiful earls the English have done badly by the rest of the nation.

But admitting that the English have produced beautiful earls—and they have—although here and there, even among earls and countesses, the national passion for projecting teeth, elongated necks, and hands and feet that do not quite match, has got the better of the equal national passion for creating and maintaining the best-looking and best-dressed upper class extant—but admitting that the English have produced beautiful earls, that is not saying that recently the richer French and Americans, especially since they have all taken to sport, have not begun to overtake the original model.

Other things being equal, all you have to do to look like an earl is to indulge in plenty of exercise, not worry overmuch, and change your clothes frequently, and the Frenchman and American have certain initial advantages—the Frenchman is more graceful, the American actually is stronger.

Many people overlook the latter fact and fail to connect it with the charge, yearly becoming less just, that although the American has the most expensive clothes in the world he does not, with a few notable exceptions, know how to wear them. Clothes made in the English fashion are made for tall thin men, not for the American physique. When the American evolves his own styles, which he is doing, and has learned to make his rounder muscles more supple, as he is learning to do, there will be less to be said on this subject. Also, another fact overlooked is that whenever the Englishman or Frenchman think of dress they think of it only in terms of the richer classes, while the American thinks of it in terms that are universal.

The American expects all Americans to look charming and is affronted when they do not. Below the upper classes, no Englishman or Frenchman imagines himself well dressed, and he most certainly isn't; but all Americans are secretly anxious to look—not like earls, but dukes. Some day most of them may.

We have spent a good deal of time on sartorial and physical matters, not only because they are important in themselves but because they form so large a share of the discontent of the apologetic American; but there is not the slightest intention of neglecting or under-emphasizing what a man thinks and does—two factors that are, of course, bound up together, but not completely. There is always a gap between what a man thinks and what he does, and in any nation, a formidable chasm between what the best minds desire and what, in action, the nation appears to be. Heaven help the world if this were not so! At all events, let us see what the Europeans and apologetic Americans accuse us of doing.

We are, to begin with, jazz-mad, motor-mad, money-mad, size-mad, crowd-mad, publicity-mad, and speed-mad. We have no privacy, no service, no time to think. If a queen comes to see us, our curiosity is inhuman; but when crowds line the streets of London every time royalty drives through, even if it only be such a remote potentate as the Emir of Afghanistan, that is merely patriotism.* According to Doctor Joseph Collins, that well-known socio-fictionist, or fictional sociologist, we are a nation of nervous invalids suffering from adult infantilism. All the evils that are now sweeping Europe are due to us; the French parsimony—to give it an ornamental name—the English vulgarity, the Charleston, the black bottom, the cheap

*The recent demonstrations accorded Mr. Ford on his bemused European trip, would seem to indicate that whereas the American worshipped birth, the European worshipped money. As a matter of fact, they indicate nothing at all save the idle idiocy of 90 per cent of any population.

motor-car, the motion-picture, the radio, road advertising, the increasingly bad manners of the Parisian waiter and the increasingly high wages of the London butler. Financially, socially, morally, and artistically, we are the source of all contagion. When the franc goes down we are to blame; when the franc goes up we are equally culpable. When we invade Europe in hordes, as we do every summer, we raise prices, consume products to the detriment of the natives, and spoil manners; when we stay away from Europe we are responsible for the empty restaurants and the near-panic that follows.

Gilbert Chesterton, in the large manner that is his, says that the disease of to-day is Americanism, and that the main object of the present generation should be to fight this disease in all its manifestations. Aldous Huxley claims that we call undertakers morticians, which we do not, except for a few pompous souls who in England would call themselves chirurgeons by appointment to His Majesty the King, or something similar, and therefore he does not like us. H. G. Wells announces that we speak and are hampered by an almost unintelligible lingo. St. John Ervine, despite the Civil War, despite some other war every ten years or so, despite pioneering and the fact that in our veins broods all the suffering of Europe up to a century or so ago, claims that we cannot produce a national drama until we pass through fire. And even John Galsworthy, that gentle critic, in his latest book created an American the like of whom has never existed on sea or land—a dinosaur of an American. This, when Galsworthy knows America intimately.

Turning to a few of our home critics, H. L. Mencken never speaks of us except as "a nation of boobs"; his playmate, that distinguished ratiocinator, George Jean Nathan, ascends Mount Sinai constantly; and Sinclair Lewis is assured that when he writes of Main Street and Babbitt and Elmer Gantry he has painted complete pictures.

Extraordinary all this—if true. What becomes of all the quiet well-bred people one knows, and the quiet beautiful homes they live in, or all the quiet homely folk who raise wheat and potatoes, and so on? One wonders at times how we even find the privacy and leisure to perpetuate the race. I think what all these gentlemen are objecting to is democracy, not America. With many of their objections no fault can be found; their error lies in their choice of a scapegoat.

We are living in an age of growing democracy, and this despite such surface reactions as the Russian commune and Mussolini. Much of the ugliness that annoys us—the breakdown in morals, in manners, the congestion, the speed, the noise, the apparently growing powers of stupidity—is due to this fact. We may not like these portents; we may try to control them, satirize them, hasten their emergence into something more comely, but we cannot prevent them. They represent evolution—never a pretty thing. We may not even believe in democracy as an ultimate political vehicle, but we shall have to endure it until we can think of something better. When you have put a man in possession of print, the motion-picture, radio and rapid communication—and even the Balkan peasants today are in possession of all four—you have made of him a potential democrat; and it makes not the slightest difference whether for a while you choose to govern him by means of an emperor, a dictator or a committee. Your only possible next step is to try to show this new democrat that democracy, if properly understood, is as brave and gentle and courteous as the best features of the lopsided thing he has left behind. Democracy is everywhere, even in the Kingdom of the Dragon. If the evils of which we speak come from America, it is only because America is further along the road, or the Via Dolorosa, or whatever you choose to call it, of the democratic pilgrimage.

Indeed, here is the amusing end of such a train of thought. Since democracy, crippled and distorted and misunderstood as it may be, is the social manifestation of the times, America, one of the youngest of nations, but one of the oldest of democracies, will, before long, of necessity find itself of all nations the most mature socially and politically. One's grandfather may be eighty-four and still be a child when it comes to running a motor-car; and although we are children where kings are concerned, we are old and sometimes even weary when presidents are in question.

And I think actual proofs of what I am saying are increasingly evident. Disease cannot sweep a nation unless a nation is ready for it. If the Europeans did not like the black bottom, they would not dance the black bottom. There must be something rotten in the souls of the French and English and Germans and Italians, or else there must be something stirring. Furthermore, you may have noticed that the European becomes enthusiastic over the Charleston and the black bottom and other American importations only when the American himself is weary of them and has gone on to something more attractive . . . or more hideous.

If a large section of the French population were not kindly disposed toward the road sign, road signs would not now be rearing their ugly heads all over France, nor would the earnest business men engaged in this sort of ruthlessness speak of France as the most hopeful European field. Even the little Thank You's and Come Again's and You Are Now Entering Col des Quatre—Chemins de l'Oie are prevalent. Meanwhile America is getting tired of road signs and is taking steps to abolish them. Note this: There is much loveliness to be seen in Europe, and an infinite amount of interest, but practically all European loveliness is old and practically all European newness is hideous. Europe may have taken the black bottom from America, but only the modern Frenchman, considering what he inherited, could have made the lovely Biarritz coast into what it is to-day.

We are, indeed, a nation of boobs, but so is every other nation; and when we consider solely action and the more material manifestations of the mind, such as architecture and landscape planning and national parks, and so on, ignorant as we are, we are nevertheless the only nation extant, save Canada, which exhibits a large intelligence. We at least know what we have done and are doing, and are pretty generally worried about it.

Expatriation is usually a sign of a middle-class mind and invariably of an unthinking mind, which does not mean that a man may not live all his life in Europe or America, and even change his citizenship, and still be unexpatriated, nor, on the other hand, that many expatriates may never have seen Europe save for a week or two. New York is full of the latter. By an expatriate I mean a man or a woman who, living out of, or in, his or her country, hates it, despises it, makes no effort to understand it, and sees only its vices, never its virtues. If that is not a description of a middle-class mind, I don't know what is. In a democracy these middle-class minds, as I hope to point out later in another paper, have no obvious standards or checks to which to relate themselves. There is no one except themselves to tell them how middle class they are. They may honestly believe the nonsense they talk; living among the vulgar clever or the vulgar rich, they may honestly think that all Americans are one or the other. Probably the hardest thing to be in the world is an intelligent democrat. As for myself, I have pursued this phantom of sophistication and good breeding into many countries and into many capitals, and I have found it rare everywhere, but as likely to be met with in Seattle as in Paris.

And this brings us to the last main factor—the factor of thought. "And here," say the apologetic Americans, "we have you. Surely you will admit, if you are honest, that compared to Europe we are distressingly young and immature in the things of the mind—where the mind functions æsthetically, where the mind functions morally." Well, I am not so sure. In this, as in other things, I think the best simile is one I recently heard—that Europe is a boy in his last year at Eton and America is a freshman at a university.

Now we all know that a boy in his last year at Eton, or any other great preparatory school, is, on the surface, a mature and finished product, while, to the contrary, the freshman is an unripe and gawky individual. Yet in reality the freshman is older. The preparatory-school boy is the climax of one system, the freshman the beginning of another, and the latter system may be an advance upon the former. The European has a façade that disturbs and embarrasses the American, and yet behind that façade there is frequently nothing but an old lady knitting socks which do not fit. Beautiful socks, delicately made, but they do not fit.

Say war to a European. He will smile, he will shrug his shoulders—all but a few young Englishmen and women—and he will leave you with the impression that you are a crass unfledged optimist to entertain for a single moment the idea that war is not inevitable. There is practically no argument against the statement: "But, you see, I am older than you." Such a statement, however, is no argument at all, and the American is not young in believing that war is nonsense and can be abolished; to the contrary, he is mature. The boy at Eton may think war cannot be abolished, but the freshman at the university knows better, although his proofs may not be so convincing.

It is always easier to prove something that has happened than it is to prove something untried. Next to European diplomacy, war is the most childish pursuit imaginable. If Europe could grow up, which it does not seem to be able to do, tomorrow we would see the forming of the United States of Europe, with its lack of tariff walls and its lack of armaments—except those directed toward the United States of North and South America. In a thousand years or so we might even see the United States of the World.

Weariness is never a sign of maturity; it is invariably a sign of callow youth or else of senility. To say *cui bono* is unreasonable. The logical conclusion of that is suicide. The vigorous point of view of which Europe accuses us is not the point of view of adolescence but the point of view of a busy and healthy man between thirty and fifty. Nor do the really intelligent Europeans ever make this blunder. It is not the really intelligent Europeans who say that we are immature because we are optimistic. The really intelligent Europeans envy us and wish that the bulk of their own nations felt the same way.

In the present state of mankind I do not believe that any one is really mature socially or morally or intellectually, but if it comes to a question of comparison, the American, it seems to me, holds his own—fundamentally, that is to say, and even where surface manners are concerned, when you consider the civilized American. I do not know any one more civilized, more charming, than the civilized American, save perhaps the civilized Frenchman. Not only in these respects does the present-day American hold his own, but the signs of growth are in him more evident than elsewhere.

Intelligent kindness is the height of sophistication; the eighteenth century, the most sophisticated century the world has ever known, was full of this sort of kindness, and the civilized American is an essentially kind creature. He has not, as a rule, time to be anything else. It is in his point of view about war and in his social contacts that he is a more noticeably mature person than the European—always, in the latter respect, although not in the former, omitting the Frenchman.

Living in a large and democratic country, where you may be a prince in Topeka but unknown as such in Philadelphia, the American has learned to judge a man minus credentials and to make himself readily accessible to every one. Does this delicate social sense seem to you immature? To the contrary, the English fear of meeting some one you shouldn't appeals to me as an excessively juvenile proceeding, a tiresome proceeding, an irritating proceeding. It is always wasteful to make a man hate you; it is much more grown up to spend a moment in politeness and then go about your business, if that be best.

Nor am I any more impressed by the Continental attitude toward sex, nor the European attitude toward art, religion, education or life in general. For every one of our follies there is an equal one abroad; although, of course, these questions should be discussed class by class; nor is it fair to match the follies of America against the follies of all Europe. One certain nation should be chosen. Very well; let us choose what is generally admitted to be the most civilized nation in existence—France.

Class by class, I should say that France and America compare as follows: In culture and intelligence and ability to enjoy life, the French upper class probably leads the world; but this does not imply that the American upper class, where these matters are in question, does not equal the English upper class and is not ahead of the German and Italian upper classes. Coming to the middle classes and the working class, the American Babbitt, as our superior fellow citizens like to call him, narrow-minded and irritating as he frequently is, is about 60 per cent more broad-minded, civilized and intelligent than the French Babbitt. He is better dressed, better informed, cleaner and infinitely less static. To see Babbittry at its blackest, cultivate the acquaintance of a small business man in a small French town; to find a narrowness and a social cruelty exceeding that of Main Street, frequent some Place de la République. While as to the American mechanic, compared with his French brother, he is a very angel of diligence and cleverness. There is not time to prove these statements, nor others I shall make; look into them for yourself.

I deprecate exceedingly, for instance—making a hasty and incomplete summary—the American legislative mind, if it can be called a mind; but I do not overlook the fact that while we have passed a law in Tennessee prohibiting the teaching of evolution, France for years has had a law prohibiting the mention of the Bible or the name of God in its public schools. What is the difference basically? Several of our states have laws against cigarettes, but all France has a law against the wearing of monastic costumes. The atheist, as we all know, is the same person as the Puritan turned upside down. And even when it comes to blue laws, France has its full quota of anti-alcohol societies, societies for cleansing the stage and societies for this, that and the other, besides its government, which is constantly passing absurd legislation to which the French, like ourselves, pay no heed. The hatred of women smoking is even more prevalent in the French middle class than in the American middle class, and the average American woman is infinitely freer than her French sister. Furthermore, just as in this country, when the popular interest in nudity and pornography is waning, as it always will if left to itself, some Parisian manager calls to his aid some society dedicated to purity, and much ado, amounting to nothing, is made. Then the sale of tickets goes up again. No, countries are not so different.

Even on the subject of sex liberty, that battle-cry so dear to the Continental and the expatriated American, I am not greatly impressed. The average French family has much the same ideas as the average American family, and the average French wife or husband is just as likely to shoot an erring spouse, and the average French court just as likely to bring in a verdict of the unwritten law, as any one hundred per cent American wife, husband or jury. While, when it comes to the upper classes, it seems to me that instead of having achieved liberty they have merely got themselves into a blind alley. Modern scientific thought, psychoanalytical and biological, points rather to the conclusion that monogamy, even if badly maintained, is a more mature ideal than polygamy perfectly practised.

Nor need we even regret the latter so long as our divorce courts remain amiable.

I am not approving either the American or French ideas of sex morality, I am merely saying that neither nation as yet has found any rational solution.

And now we come to what is generally considered the final test of a nation's maturity, the production and reproduction of art, although I am by no means convinced that this is so. The Swedes, I am sure, are an extremely intelligent, sensitive and advanced people, and yet artistically they are not especially articulate. The Romans were a mature people, but they were not artistic. The English are a mature people, and yet they have always been singularly lacking in every art save the art of country living and the arts of the written word—prose and poetry. They not only have been lacking—they have been viciously inartistic. But suppose we agree with the common belief; if we do I do not see that we suffer by comparison.

Of the four fairly great playwrights alive today, one is an American, O'Neill, one an Italian, Pirandello, one an Irishman, Shaw, and one an Hungarian, Molnar. In the second flight, perhaps some day to be the first, what with Sydney Howard, Marc Conolly, and so on, we are above the rest of the world. There is only one great poet, and he happens, as is usually the case, to be an Englishman—Masefield. There is no really supreme novelist, but in this respect we are maintaining our own and steadily improving. Willa Cather, Hergesheimer, Ernest Hemingway, Dreiser, Ellen Glasgow, Cabell, Anne Parish, are a fairly shining galaxy, to mention only a few. The last great English novelist, if we except Hardy who survived until recently but ceased novel writing long ago, was, of course, a Pole.

In painting and sculpture, since there is an interregnum in greatness, there are few to be compared, and the same holds true of music; but in the rank and file of these arts, and in the promises held forth, we are at a high level, while among our great dead are St. Gaudens, Whistler, Sargent and McDowell. In the arts of architecture and medicine we are obviously not immature, while in the reproduction of all the arts we have suddenly leaped into first place. This, of course, is natural. We are the richest nation in the world, therefore we will begin first to reproduce more beautifully than any other; secondly, to teach more adequately, and finally to produce more gorgeously. This is the history of all great nations. Years ago, before our English cousins began to misunderstand us as blindly as they do at present, Lowes Dickinson predicted within a few decades just such a renaissance, and to-day signs are everywhere evident.

But I will close my categories for lack of space; I will leave my theories for others to develop. We are children, all of us; we are mongrels, all of us. For America I claim no superiority; there is no intentional chauvinism here; I am excessively humble about the faults of America and Americans. I detest these faults more than most. I am merely asking for fair-mindedness, merely, to use an excellent locution, asking for an even break—something that America at present is not getting either from Europe or from many Americans. Particularly, I am asking this from Americans, for they should know better. Perhaps the day for their knowing better is dawning.

The growing European dislike of us—a dislike that has spread even to Belgium, whom we picked up out of the mud—internationally is a tragedy, but for us domestically it may be a blessing. If the apologetic American is kicked about sufficiently, even he or she may achieve after a while some degree of quiet dignity.

III

HOKUM

III

HOKUM

THERE are certain fundamental events, and spiritual and physiological processes, that happen to every one, and these happen even to Broadway producers, motion-picture stars, gold-digging chorus girls, columnists, flappers, college seniors, recent millionaires, and the youthful sardonicists of the critical world of New York or the world of the immature university. Among these events are being born, dying, and to every one who survives to fifteen, or, as the psycho-analysists now tell us, who survives beyond a few months, the being attracted by a member of the opposite sex, whether the last take shape merely as the cacodemon of lust or the half angel, half bird we hear about but seldom see. These things happen and there is no avoiding them. In fact, life stripped of its ormolu is so exceedingly stark that fiction has only nine, or eleven, basic plots—the exact number has never been determined.

But humanity does not like starkness, it is the

one thing humanity can not abide, so artistically and socially, and in all other ways of course, save for narrow interregnums of actual revolution, the history of the human race has been a history of concerted attempts to cover up or deny, by this fashion or that, the common fate. Cromwell tried to do this by prayer and persecution, the playwrights of the Restoration by laughter. The pendulum swings backward and forward and only for the second when it is in the exact axial position between the two extremes do we even begin to approach the truth. In other words, the philosophy of the more egregious modern maidens, and of Oxford bags is as far removed from reality as the philosophy of vapors and smelling salts. The atheist is quite as mad as the fundamentalist, and hard-boiled youth is only the reverse of soft-boiled senility.

The examples of these phenomena do not like each other, and do not understand each other when they meet, but both have, if they but knew it, an underlying bond of excessive sentimentality. Both are attempting to disclaim life.

Several gentle old ladies of my acquaintance will not mention the word cancer; any number of young, or youngish, people of my acquaintance will not mention the word beauty. The little boys and girls, too frank and modern to be polite, are merely expressing in current terms the bland egotism expressed by their grandmothers and grandfathers through an elaborate subterfuge of courtesy. The Victorians took more trouble over their selfishness, that is all. The exact truth, in this particular instance, would be, of course, simple good manners. Between denying, or embellishing, a fact because it is supposed to be too ugly, as the Victorians did, and denying a fact because it is supposed to be too pretty, or too banal, as many moderns do, there is intrinsically not the slightest difference. As if facts were ever anything but banal! . . . Or exciting. Depending upon the way you look at them.

At all events, it happens that just at present we are in an excellent position to study this circular and not especially gainful process, for we are just emerging from one well-defined period and, after a few years of actual but, as always, confused and fairly grotesque rebellion, seem to be on the point of entering another period that shows signs of being equally well-defined. Having destroyed the lollipops of the Victorians, we have our mouths greedily set for lollipops of our own. And, most important, we have suddenly come to the conclusion that we are sophisticated and that, of course, is the exact moment when gold-bricks are likely to be sold to us. The suspicious rustic is seldom in danger.

Hokum and buncombe, the latter distorted

into the hideous phrase, "that is the bunk," have been the rallying-cries of the released, those together with "applesauce," but from the present on we have need to be careful lest these slogans of liberation become the "prisoners' songs" of our own and the rising generation. Shibboleths are dangerous the moment they lose their original careful interpretation. Freedom, once codified, is tyranny. The Black Mass is just as elaborate, as time-taking, as demanding as the mass it seeks to supplant. It is possible to imagine a future in which embattled monogamists will furnish auto da fés for serious and convinced polygamists who will weep and pray over them as Philip of Spain did over his heretics.

Let us see what has happened to us in the last twenty years.

According to our notions the Victorians, and this means in most cases our grandparents, and in many cases our parents, despite their powerful impulses and accomplishments, lived in a world of illusion which it has been our duty—and pleasure—to destroy. This, fairly well accomplished, we have emerged into the clearer atmosphere of to-day. Possibly. One does not deny the illusions of the Victorians, one merely questions the clearer atmosphere of to-day. Or rather, not of to-day, for the atmosphere actually does seem clearer, but of tomorrow. We have not as yet left altogether the interregnum of revolution, so some of our revolution is still valid, but we are beginning to bow and scrape before the royal feet of new chimeras.

The essential error of the Victorians lay not so much in a denial of fact, for that was resorted to only when there was nothing else to be done, as in the assumption that most facts were ugly and therefore needed decoration. Our essential error is likely to lie in a belief that a fact is not a fact unless it is unpleasant, and that most facts aren't worth bothering about anyway. With the Victorians, facts were corsetted, bejewelled, tight-booted, and long-skirted. In verse they were put into the sonorous rhythms of the iambic pentameter and in prose there was a collusion of delicate evasion. There was even a period when one addressed one's wife as "Mrs." and when the human body was never seen in its entirety, not even by its owner, save by the doctor at birth and the undertaker at death. This, naturally, was unbearable and the forthright and courageous began to attack such a point of view even before it became duly accredited.

Where suppression is the protagonist on the one hand and liberty of thought the protagonist on the other, the primary object of the early revolutionist is to get things said; to use exact words and to state positively and clearly that such and such things exist and such and such things do not. The principal crippling of the Victorian mind lay in the fact that a quarter of the magnificent vocabulary of the English language was not admitted to polite usage. And if you deny words you deny facts, for words follow upon facts and each word expresses a fact. Nowadays, thanks to these early revolutionists, all words, save a very few, are permissible both in print and speech, and that is as it should be, but, having achieved our point, we are on the way to forget once again that nothing—not even words or facts—is in this world removed from the qualifying factors of circumstances and intention; that there is nothing, in short, isolated from its immediate environment.

There is practically nothing that cannot be said if the circumstances and the intention are correct, there is practically nothing that should be said if the circumstances and the intention are wrong. The mere desire to shock is as sentimental as the mere desire to suppress. We have all heard people say God in a way that made our hair creep and we have all heard people use indecency in a way that warmed our hearts. There is not much sense in destroying a fiction if we erect another in its place. To be educated out of reading *The Fireside Companion* into reading, let us say, *College Wit,* is to be educated out of the kitchen by a circuitous route back to the butler's pantry.

The Victorians did not like to speak of death because they thought death ugly and it affronted their pompous dignity, therefore they called it "passing on," or "facing one's Maker," or "the final moment"—circumlocutions which meant nothing. We do not like to speak of death, because it is interrupting and affronts our restless exhibitionism, therefore we say "getting his," or "passing out" or, if we belong to a lower social order, "bumped off"—circumlocutions which also mean nothing. The fierce intention of the early revolutionists was to get the word *death* back into the language, that and nothing else, in the same way that their fierce intention was to restore the human body to its frank and commendable reality. But mankind is not content with equilibrium, or even a vague approach to it—for the human body is not yet, of course, restored to its frank and commendable reality—so it leaps numerous unbridged chasms from one pinnacle of nonsense to another. To the Victorian mind the legs of all women were indecent and ugly, to the modern mind the legs of all women are supposed to be decent and comely. In either case the sensitive-minded suffer.

The fact that marriage is not the romantic hypocrisy of the Victorians, with its outer soft syllables and its inner harsh words, its perversions and inversions, its lunatic asylum as the one recourse of the unhappy, does not mean that it is, to the contrary, the temporary affair it so often is to-day. The Victorian who lied about marriage and said it was made in heaven was no more soft-headed or sentimental, no farther from the starkness of truth, than the uneasy rebel, the rich idler, or the motion-picture star who lie about marriage and say it is made in Reno. And the essential similarity is proven by the truth that the insane asylum is frequently still the only refuge. When you mix your categories you end in confusion, just as the artist ends in confusion when he essays to mix his mediums. Marriage is one thing, free love is another, divorce is a third. There is much to be said for and against each one, but when you attempt to achieve free love by means of marriage plus divorce you achieve nothing, neither the advantages of a wife nor a mistress. Instead, you merely achieve a succession of mistresses each one with the exigeant rights of a wife. The truth is not even approached. A lady who breaks up a household evades the issue when the breaking ends in another marriage and need not comfort herself with the thought of morality.

But hokum is a much more subtle and permeating essence than is visible in these already well-worn instances. Like the first gas attack during the war, it looks to the unwarned no more than a creeping yellow mist on the horizon, until, pretty soon, they are strangling to death in its midst. If you fall into the habit of denying all specifications of a certain kind you are all too likely to acquire the habit of proclaiming all specifications of another kind. The brilliance that enables you to perceive that geese are not swans may lead you, unless you are wise as well, into the shadow where all swans look like geese. It is an easy game to play. You choose a noun or an adjective and then state its antonym. The equipment of most up-to-date critics is simple and light; it consists of Roget's "Thesaurus."

Let's begin.

Discipline, free will; romance, reality; beauty, ugliness; religion, atheism; lyric, vers libre; melody, cacophony; banal, original; Victorian, modern; older generation, younger generation; hypocrisy, frankness. Without intricate, subtle, and hard-minded investigation each one of these terms means just as much as the other and the users haven't as a rule the faintest idea what they are talking about. Black fades into white and human life is delicately shaded, it is by no means susceptible to such sweeping generalizations. But the game of antonyms is fascinating and one distinguished critic is at present conducting a campaign against bird-songs solely, as far as can be made out, because most people take pleasure in them.

We are creating a most elaborate hokum of our own and the emergence of this can best be seen, perhaps, in our literature and stage, for these two mediums are the first to respond to rebellion and the first to succumb to illusions newly evolved. To the ancient hokum of "Abie's Irish Rose" a section of the advanced stage has responded gallantly, and the hokum of those of the clergy, especially those who conduct columns in the public prints and who settle in a few sentences the fate of the world, is ably matched by the hokum of the radical novelist who says that nothing can be settled at all. The heart of hokum is the denial of the truth and it makes no difference how you deny it. The hokum of radicalism is the twin brother of the hokum of reaction. Both arise from a conviction that every one else save yourself is a fool. The intelligent radical and the intelligent satirist never fall into the error of minimizing the intrinsic worth that must originally have been in the platform of their opponents. They attack not so much humanity—no, not even Dean Swift—as the evil ways into which humanity falls. To heap contempt, for instance, upon the so-called "service clubs" *per se* is not radicalism but class prejudice, since these so-called service clubs are the response to a powerful need of a certain type of human mind. Criticism should be reserved for the absurd and venal practices which overtake such clubs.

No wise religious radical laughs at Jesus Christ —or Mahomet, if you prefer that—for if he does he shows himself, if nothing else, ignorant of history and the secret places of the heart. Instead, he attacks the base perversions of the church.

Or, if you believe all religion evil, then you should attack religion itself, not the hypocritical lives of a small section of the clergy. At the best, the latter method only makes numerous people angry and confirms others in what they already know. A Reverend Frank Norris does not invalidate a Cardinal Manning. Dishonest bankers do not prove banking unnecessary. If most of our sorrows are due to banking itself, and many people think so, then attack the whole capitalistic system, as Marx did, and do not waste your ammunition on trivialities. As Rebecca West says, to discover and drag out into the limelight of scorn an old lady in Iowa who has read her Bible a hundred times is as if Voltaire had lost his breath deriding the pietistic practices of Breton peasants. Furthermore, the game within a short time becomes absolute hokum, for it is so easy that you can play it blindfolded and automatically, and what you are doing is to convince yourself and others that an entirely natural impulse amongst old ladies is some sort of tortuous mendacity.

All through time old ladies have read their Bibles, or sacrificed to Baal, or whatever it was, as an expression of their sense of the near approach of death. What you should do, if you want to do something important, is to so train young women that when they become old ladies they will read their Bibles, or sacrifice to Baal, with some degree of intelligence. To leave a vacuum is merely to create a playground for windy devils. The similarity between a meeting of the average Kiwanis Club and the average gathering of the intelligentsia is appalling, leaving the open-minded spectator open-mouthed with amazement.

To destroy all existing human beliefs, fatuous as they may be, only to substitute in their place a frank code of rape, drunkenness, and verbal obscenity is in the end not even to substitute frankncss for hypocrisy. All ages that have tried this code have speedily found themselves in a maze of formalized indecency. I refer you to Petronius and his "Satyricon" as an example.

Hokum, after all, is largely the failure to react normally. The Victorians failed to react normally because they were under the spell of an elaborate code of evasion, we are beginning to fail to react normally because we are under the spell of an elaborate code of so-called elimination and honesty. We are constantly being called upon to be honest when there is nothing to be honest about. We deride the service clubs, and rightly, because they have an elaborate code of good-fellowship concealing a cold and deadly selfishness. But what is the difference between that and an elaborate code of rudeness concealing an equal selfishness? Furthermore, there are so many mechanical and artificial stimuli nowadays that we are in danger of losing most of our reactions anyway. Stevenson's prayer to be stabbed wide awake has increased in value. New York might be called the city of lost reactions, as might Paris, as far as that is concerned, or London. When a man is electrocuted his heart jumps repeatedly for several minutes if you draw a thumb-nail across it. After a while it ceases to respond. The hearts of a good many city dwellers are in the latter condition.

The clergyman, or large, cold-eyed business man, who announces that all is for the best in the best possible of worlds is no greater purveyor of hokum than the sleek young translator or producer who claims that perversion—let us say—has become so common a factor in life that it has assumed the largeness necessary for tragedy. And this is so whether the claim is based on venal hypocrisy or the fact that a translator or producer has reached the point where he responds only to abnormal stimuli. Beautiful and tragic things may be said about perversion, and in one instance recently they have been said, but it is an old and proven rule that nothing can be warm food, except for experts of life, until it has some elements of the universal; up to that time it is dangerous for the larger public and generally popular for no artistic reasons. Nor is this contradicting the well-taken stand of the pscho-analysists that everything is universal. Undoubtedly everything is, but until a particular thing is actively present in the common consciousness, if treated publicly at all, it must be treated as the universal workings of a blind Fate, as the Greeks treated such subjects, and not as the particular horrors of an individual or small group, no matter how splendidly conceived and executed the history may be.

The classic attitude, after all, is the only one as yet discovered that is a sure cure for sentimentality, or, in other words, hokum.

The arrival of our own brand of hokum has been hastened, moreover, and our susceptibility to it heightened, by a peculiar and not clearly recognized reinforcement in the shape of the increasing influence of orientalism upon Western nations.

The Oriental has much to commend him, but he belongs to a tired race, he actually has eliminated. Unfortunately his elimination has been in a direction entirely opposed to any possible future and much-to-be-desired elimination on the part of the Occidental. The desire of the Occidental, despite how little most Occidentals think and how little the desire is evident, is always toward spiritual and intellectual elimination—toward the sparse, clear regions of the mind and a concentrated warmth of emotion. The Oriental—that is, the particular Oriental of whom I am speaking—persecuted and confined, has learned to eliminate in the direction of texture, and the sensation of the moment, or the sensation that will arise from a single-eyed pursuit of an especial, not-too-hard-to-obtain end. In short, the elimination of everything except that which can be packed up and carried off, in the mind or in boxes, in the face of impending pogroms, or that which can be carried on from a distance, or put aside and readily taken up again once the pogroms cease. The Oriental, in other words—all Orientals, as a matter of fact, save the East Indian—and possibly the East Indian as well, since Nirvana is no more than a symbol of a philosophy born of overcrowding—is a pragmatist. When the Oriental finds himself surrounded by Occidentals he exercises his peculiar talents by catering, with his tongue in his cheek, to what he thinks is the sentimentality of his neighbors. His mental reservations are sardonic. Or else, if he is a rarely powerful and honest Oriental, he seeks to impose upon an alien audience, and educate them to, a set of reactions not their own. He misunderstands the Occidental as the Occidental misunderstands him.

Save in the Mediterranean basin, where he has long been under Oriental influence, the Occidental cannot and never will recover from the perhaps altogether illogical belief that beyond everything there is an indefinable creature called the soul; the Oriental, to the contrary, is as dry and pragmatic as the desert winds that once blew upon him. Forced by the common ambition to make money, the Occidental, for instance, will hire hundreds of young women to dash out on a stage in a state of comparative nudity before hundreds of one hundred per cent American travelling salesmen, but, believing that all these young girls have souls, which is doubtful, he will weep about his action and lie to himself. The Oriental has no such pangs and will lie only to meet the requirements of the Occidental—requirements he thinks, mistakenly, are hypocritical. He does not care whether the young women have souls or not so long as their bodies form a colorful and desirable pattern. He has no conception of the dual Occidental personality which is constantly agonizing in a world where, in order to make a living, one has frequently to break all the rules of life.

He has no idea of the God of the old Scotch dominie, who in his official and public capacity performs many an act he must be ashamed of as a private citizen.

But you can see how the juxtaposition of such differing points of view makes at once for hokum; the hokum of the pragmatist playing up to what he thinks a sentimentalist wants, or, at the other end of the scale, the hokum of a sentimentalist, vaguely uneasy about his sentimentality and unable to separate it from his genuine sentiment, trying to play up to the opinions of a pragmatist. At all events, both are bad for art, which is a bitter attempt to ascertain the truth. And that the Occidental, whatever his faults, is a better artist than his rival is proven, it seems to me, by artistic history. A better final artist, that is; not a better performer, perhaps, or producer. The Oriental is an excellently chromatic background, but otherwise artistic history is filled with extinguished Oriental comets.

You have to be a bit of a fool to be a great artist. You have to forget yourself and give yourself away at times. You have to be a trifle uncertain and, above all, you cannot deny mystery. This, as a member of an audience, is interesting to watch. When an audience comes forward psychically toward a great artist, whether he be a fiddler, an actor, a painter, a singer, a novelist, a composer or a poet, inevitably the great artist comes forward to meet his audience. The two mingle and ascend by alternate reactions toward an indefinable and, possibly, sentimental apex. But the Oriental cannot do this. He is always a *Nitouche*, as he is in his personal relationships, stepping back out of the picture, a frightened or amused smile on his lips. He has not the final silliness—if you wish to call it that—of the transcendent creator.

And so we come, as we must in any discussion of this kind, to the greatest purveyor of modern hokum there is, that curiously orientalized, wrongly sophisticated, evilly demure creature, the motion-picture—the most widely influential of the arts, if it can be called an art, which I am quite sure as yet it cannot be. The motion-picture has a curious hokum of its own, far more subtle than the apparent hokum assigned to it. It is not the comparatively simple reverse-English of much of the radical stage and radical literature, nor is it in reality a frankly cynical appeal to banality, although that is what for the most part it is intended to be. The peculiar and mistaken sophistication of the people who make motion-pictures is such that with them frank and not unwholesome banality is impossible. The motion-pictures have a reverse reverse-English; you box the compass, passing through vast realms of pseudo-sophistication—or perhaps real sophistication, for the term originally had no complimentary meaning—and arrive finally at nothing. But on the way many of the more unpleasant traces of sophistication are caught by the skirts of the bathing-girl muse. Due to censorship, the average present-day motion-picture represents a tacit conspiracy on the part of the public and the producers to agree that all ends well if it ends in matrimony. In between you can titillate all you want. You can suggest and fade-out or cut-back to any sort of monstrosity you prefer. And—after all—the nudity or escapades of another man's wife, or husband, are not such personal or accustomed matters as not to titillate. Sadism, for example, between young people formally affianced is no different than sadism between comparative strangers—at least, not to the casual spectators. A young lady in a cube root minus bathing-suit, even if in the final close-up she indicates her intention to marry the hero, is still a young lady in a cube root minus bathing-suit except to the hardened judges of beauty contests and those simple souls who insist that display eventually produces a charming anæsthesia regarding the female figure. Every other art having striven for decades to prove that marriage means nothing in itself and is frequently a most immoral convention, the motion-pictures are claiming that marriage means everything and is a cloak for all evil.

But there is another conspiracy of which the motion-picture producers are unaware that will one day bankrupt the original conspiracy, an unconscious conspiracy in which the audience is an enforced participant. And this is proven by the fact that nowadays wherever an audience is partially civilized it is necessary to introduce dancing and music, and various other adventitious props, to support the tottering edifice. Not one person engaged in the making of motion-pictures believes in a single premise connected with the vast majority of the pictures they make, the only premise they believe in—one common to the partially wise and rashly educated—is that their pictures are being made for audiences of morons. They cannot get through their heads that most people are not really morons, and that after a while, if you persist, you can insult even stupid people intellectually. They may be ill-informed, these people, ignorant, obstinate, and prejudiced, but they are not morons. Meanwhile, lacking other amusement, and in the habit of seeking some sort of recreation, say Tuesday and Friday nights, the outlying public permits in silence the whims of the producers, even to permitting that final insult and, as far as the pictures are concerned, new form of megalomania, where the leading characters of a story bear the first names of the leading actors and at times the actors even step out of their medium and, in their ordinary street clothes and personalities, appear on the screen.

It will be interesting to see what happens when the lure of doing something on Tuesday and Friday nights fails any longer to function. It will be interesting when the audience begins to educate the producers.

During the next twenty years the coming generation of radicals and haters of hokum will have their hands full. Perhaps among the first of their startling and terrifying pronouncements will be the battle-cry that all women, possibly unfortunately, do not kiss you the first time they see you, and that "Ulysses" is not a complete picture of the average man's mind. It may even be that a renewed interest will be taken in those inevitably important but at present entirely unconsidered members of society, the gently bred man and woman, if for no other reason than because, no matter what may be said to the contrary, they of all people are the least given to hokum.

IV

FUROR BRITANNICUS

IV

FUROR BRITANNICUS

****

IV

FUROR BRITANNICUS

I CHOOSE Mr. Wells—H. G. Wells—as my hero for reasons I will immediately explain, although nowadays it is possible to choose any one of threescore others. Mr. Wells is suffering from a form of monomania. The particular monomania with which he is afflicted has been for a century or more so common among his countrymen as to be, until recently, hardly worthy of note. One has sighed and regarded it as inevitable. But lately this monomania has taken a dangerous turn, and in Mr. Wells's case it is different anyhow.

To begin with, on so many subjects and for so many years, he has been right, and to end with, by temperament he is better fitted than most to understand the American scene. Did he but know it, he is the most American of English writers. When a person like Mr. Wells becomes affected, it is a sign of a national point of view so pervasive, so increasing, that intelligent and stupid are alike caught up by it. If this continues, even Hugh Walpole, one of the few friends we have left, may be counted upon to issue egregious statements; and that most courteous of men, John Drinkwater, may take to hurling jelly at the heads of his American hostesses after the fashion of still another British author of note.

Once a nation starts to enlarge a prejudice against another, there is no telling where the prejudice will end. Folly feeds on folly. Folly becomes fashionable, imperative; a question of catchwords and repeated fables. We have seen a century during which England, the most powerful of nations, has been hated on a basis mostly of lies; we are beginning a century, perhaps two or more, when America will be hated in the same way and for the same reason. International phobias, well started, do not die. It appears now, for instance, to be as necessary for a right-thinking Englishman mentally to kick a Frenchman as, in 1914, it was necessary mentally to kiss him. Mutual respect is no longer imperative for mutual safety. And the Frenchman replies by a grinning contempt.

A form of fanged and slobbering nonsense, of course. There is never a valid reason for such hatreds. No excuses save old wives' tales and superstitions and deliberate, or ignorant, misconceptions.

The articulate Englishman, therefore, has need to exercise care. Despite Mr. Wells and the newer school of transatlantic critics, Americans are human. They have feelings, even if these feelings, according to this school, are crude. Americans are mammals. Their blood is hot. The American woman still suckles her young. One and all, they bleed if you prick them. If you find yourself cherishing, for any other people as a whole, contempt or a sense of superiority or dark anger, look to yourself, for on that side of you, you are becoming a fool.

But let Mr. Wells do his own talking. He has been doing it for almost half a century. He is probably the most adept exhibitionist alive to-day. Nobody can explain him a quarter as well as he can explain himself. And mark the gist of his theory as it unfolds itself, for that is one of the minor points. It might be called "the theory of monstrosity,"—a theory becoming, where America is concerned, increasingly popular—and the psychological reasons for it are plain. It is no longer possible to look down on America materially or politically or financially, or in most other ways, but since you can't look down on America in these ways, you must find other ways to look down upon her; and above all, you must give reasons why, even in the ways you can't look down upon her, you don't want to be like her. You must interpret this abnormal increase in power so that it leaves you, as a European, satisfied. And abnormal it must be, since Americans are not Europeans and normal things do not happen outside of Europe. Very little happens outside of Europe except African war-dances and Hindus and mysterious Chinese who are acting very much as Cromwell did in the seventeenth century.

Here, then, is Mr. Wells talking on page 323 of one of his latest books, "The World of William Clissold." Mr. Wells, talking in the person of Richard, older brother of William, for, despite the introduction, in which the common error of identifying the hero of a novel, or the other characters, with the author of the novel is dwelt upon, Mr. Wells cannot help being a most personal author. Undoubtedly most of the incidents in "The World of William Clissold" are fictitious. At all events, we can accept their creator's word for that. But it is an innocent soul who cannot find, when it comes to argument, to theorizing, Mr. Wells himself peering out from behind the effigies he has set up. He enjoys debate too much to allow figments of the mind to steal his pleasure.

"Billy," says Richard—or Dickon, according to the English custom of overly affectionate nicknames—"Billy, why are Americans, all Americans, Americans without exception, such mysteries to us? European race. More often than not our race. Our language." Thank you, Mr. Wells! Quite liberal and un-English, although afterward you contradict it. "Conditions after all very like ours. A bigger country, of course. A different pace. Difference of phase. But while you seem to get Englishmen and Frenchmen all around and through and through, half an American is in a loud glare and the other half is darkness. It is like seeing things by the beam of a search-light after you have been seeing them in a light that is soft and gray and generally diffused.

"That's it, perhaps, Billy. A profound difference in their publicity, using publicity in its widest sense. From the way that a child gets looked at and talked about, onward. They're lit up differently, inside and out. And what is life but a consequence of illumination? When you go to America and see head-lines and interviews with a girl about her engagement, or with a professor about his resignation, you at first say, 'Good God. There's no privacy here at all!' And then you discover that outside that crude, cheap, hasty, flat, misleading lighting up of salient objects and events, there's abysses of darkness, immense pits where much goes on and nothing is exposed—and people, rich people especially, unobserved in them, and doing the most extraordinary things.

"In Europe a man may have a private life, yes,

but in America he has a secret life, lit by sudden shouting judgments and flashes of journalistic lightning. In which you get an impression—vivid enough but wrong. And other things come out with a kind of scream, all out of proportion by our standards. It's because of that, Billy, that to our European senses Americans never seem quite real. The quality of the exposure, the method of illumination to which they have had to adapt themselves, account for nearly everything between us. That sort of watchful reserve they have, mixed up with a desire to make general, over-simplified explanations of themselves. The queerness of these grayish-faced, slow-speaking Americans in gray, who watch your face as they talk to you! If the search-light jumps around upon them they are ready all the time. They talk about themselves as we never do."

Oh, Mr. Wells! Come, come. You, as the author of—well, you know—a hundred books or so about Mr. Wells. And what about the queer English fashion of frank, brutal statements concerning parents and families? The English fashion of complete divulgement of private sins? The Englishman who invariably says, "Well, I'm this sort of a man, y'see—" And, coming back to you once more, how about your own passion for over-simplified explanations, both of yourself and things in general, as in the present quotation? "They try and hide their nakedness behind autobiographical statements. They instance themselves as types. They snatch suddenly at your verdict upon them. They have none of our sense of sustained scrutinies and slowly maturing judgments; none at all."

For a while Dickon is compressed. The essence of Dickon is given:

"He sized up the prospects of a world under American leadership. Were the Americans producing an American mind that would be large-thinking and powerful enough for the whole world? In certain things they were broader minded than Europeans. The United States had always been more curious and intelligent about China and eastern Asia, for example, and more restrained in its imperialism. It had been far ahead of the European intelligence in its grasp of the importance of a properly regulated currency and credit system to economic life. It had got currency into politics long before Europe suspected there was such a thing as a currency riddle. But, nevertheless, it was—shallow. All its energy—and its energy was tremendous—seemed to be on the surface. Woodrow Wilson was typical of the American quality that perplexed us. The idea of some great settlement of world affairs, some world peace organization, was magnificent. Quite beyond the scope of the European outlook or the compass of European statesmanship. One saw the United States leading the world into a new age. Then, for the realization of that vision, the Fourteen Points, as trite and superficial as a magazine article.

"And after that—America the creditor."

Dickon is quoted again in whole. Dickon, or Mr. Wells. And in all honesty one must admit that Dickon, or Mr. Wells, ends in a surprising burst of fairness and good sense. There are streaks of light, after all, in the blackness of Mr. Wells's present monomania.

" 'And while we sit here asking,' says Dickon, 'can the Americans develop a world mind and lead the world?' there may be just such another pair of brothers as we are, Billy, in Indianapolis or Chicago saying, 'Why don't the Europeans show a sign of a world mind?' I believe our sort of ideas are fermenting in the world everywhere. We're not such original chaps as to be very far from the general trail. What brings us here will bring others here. And Americans most of all.

"It's just that we don't know about them. They aren't talking yet . . ."

Certainly, Dickon. And, no, you and William are not startlingly original. What made you so quaintly think you even ever a little were? There are scores of such brothers, or maybe merely cousins or acquaintances; and they are talking—talking continuously. So, too, are reviews and newspapers and committees and organizations. Although Indianapolis and Chicago are not especially happy choices as localities. The first is just at present terribly preoccupied with the Ku Klux Klan—our form of Fascism—and the latter is busy with gunmen and Mayor Thompson, while both have always belonged to the Middle West, which, of all parts of America, is the most self-contained and the least likely to be interested in international affairs. But as for America as a whole, it is indeed the most likely country to develop first a world mind, not only for a reason I will give later on but because, unbelievable as it may seem, it is the only country which does not cherish an especial hatred for any other. Prejudices, yes; ignorances, yes; but not especial hatreds. You see, you have to know America fairly intimately to criticise it at all.

Dickon, however, if you remember, was suffering from influenza. No wonder he saw long processions of grayish-faced, slow-speaking Americans. Once when I had influenza in Germany millions of fantastic Germans goose-stepped for hours across the bottom of my bed. But Mr. Wells in person is not suffering from influenza in an article of his which appeared in the New York *Times* of May 15, 1927. He is vigorous, clear-eyed, mistaken and temerarious. He praises us because recently we have taken to criticizing ourselves. Criticism is good for the soul; is a sign of increasing maturity. Quite so. But not aberrational criticism. Somewhat naïvely, the article is entitled, "Wells Assays the Culture of America."

Imagine assaying the culture of a country of this size in three thousand words! Imagine assaying the culture of any country in three thousand words. Imagine any great English journal asking an American, or any one else for that matter, to assay the culture of England. In that respect we are indeed still youthful. And here, lest my tones belie me, let me state that I am not passionate. I do not really care very much what Mr. Wells thinks—Mr. Wells or any other European critic. Long ago, like most travelling and reading Americans, I became indurate on that score. Against my real nature, I have become thick-skinned. I cannot help it if Mr. Wells cannot understand us, and I am sure that I will be unable to show him the way. Nor am I using, as I use in other of these papers, the old method of the pot and the kettle as a mere vulgar *tu quoque*. I am using it in the hope that some European, less given to snap-shot judgments than Mr. Wells may see the point.

The longer I live the more I find that human society is lateral and not perpendicular. By that I do not mean to imply that America is not producing a civilization of its own—for it is—or that Europe has not produced a civilization of its own—for it has—or that climate, circumstances, distances do not count. But fundamental human vices and virtues are much the same, and human sympathies, save in times of war, are much more a question of especial professions or environments than they are of nations. The American engineer, for instance, has much more to say to the English engineer than he has to the American actress; the gently bred American gets along extremely well with the gently bred Dane. Nor can you turn any race of men into monsters. Monsters, if there are such things, and men do not breed. Monsters are a species apart.

And so we can get back to Mr. Wells and his article. It is impossible to quote it in full, as in the case of the sayings of Dickon in "The World of William Clissold," but altogether clearly the main points come out:

America is crude. America is arid. The American promise is doubtful.

And then, as in William Clissold, once more the theory to which I have referred—the theory that America, although it has become a great and powerful nation, is producing a civilization—if you can call it that? In the European mind there is always the question, "If you can call it that?" —which is unnatural, inhuman, mechanical, and bloodless. A civilization of swarming motor-cars and minds and spirits that do not function. A civilization of robots—although Mr. Wells does not believe in robots.

And to prove his points Mr. Wells has taken as his prophets, Sinclair Lewis, Sherwood Anderson, and Theodore Dreiser; and as his textbooks, "Babbitt," "Elmer Gantry," and "An American Tragedy." Quite so; he would. Representative books, he calls them. Yes, and according to his notion, the only sort of American books that are representative. Quaint, isn't it? Exactly as if an American, in the days when Mr. Bennett and Mr. Wells were the most popular English writers in America, should have judged all England by the Five Towns and Mr. Polly, or as if an American to-day should judge all England by D. H. Lawrence and Thomas Burke. Or, to go back awhile, as if an American should judge all Victorian England by the grotesques of Dickens.

"The first quality that impresses the European," says Mr. Wells, "is the abounding vigor of the social life these books reveal. The next is its immense crudity and, hard on that, its lack of variety in culture and the absence of half shades—a sort of universal black and whiteness. Everybody seems to think the same things and express them by the same idioms." Having just reread "Limehouse Nights," I retort: "Isn't it a pity all Englishmen smoke opium and have to do with half-caste Chinese women?" And having just reread "Pickwick Papers," I say: "Isn't it odd how round and fat and absurd all Englishmen of three generations ago were?"

"Let me set down two impressions of a very intelligent French reader of these representative books," says Mr. Wells further on. "The first impression was one of the wide freedom of movement and the universal restlessness of these common people, compared with the rooted, limited lives of their European equivalents. The next and the stronger was the extreme thinness and poverty of their mental life. We were in the presence of a people with no depth of conversation at all. They had no variety nor penetration in their discussion. They had no poetry whatever. They did not seem to know the names of or ever to have observed any birds, flowers, minerals, or natural things.

"They had not metaphors, but slang phrases, horribly bent and flattened by excessive use. They betrayed nothing a European could recognize as religion and no general ideas of any sort. Their revivalism was the cheapest, shallowest orgy of mass emotion. They knew nothing of any literature. They read so badly that their news had to be shouted at them from the tops of columns. The poverty of their language was amazing. The lover wrung to ecstasy might say: 'My, but you are cute!' The phrase for all occasions seemed to be: 'That gets me!'

"My French observer insisted that here was a people degenerating, worn halfway back to speechlessness and brutishness. We had a long argument, because I am still a backer of the United States"—Thank you again, Mr. Wells!—"and in the end we both gave ground. I had to grant the flattening and cheapening of the language, but it was arguable that that is a phase. Two-thirds of the surnames in Dreiser's books were central or eastern European names. These people were newcomers; they had left Polish and Yiddish, or German behind them, and the names of flowers and legend and metaphor had also been left behind. There had been a vast mental attrition during the process of transplantation to a new soil. No real attempt had been made to assimilate them to any conceivable American culture." No more than any attempt has been made to assimilate to any conceivable English culture the swarming aliens of

London's East End, or the Irish of Liverpool, or the workers of Glasgow.

And then Mr. Wells concludes with this extraordinary hodgepodge in which there is not the slightest assimilation of any kind:

The common schools of America are on the whole not as good as those of Britain and Germany, whereas they ought to be four times better. A postulation which assumes that Americans are not only inhuman but archangels. American children are not made to go to school as regularly as the children of western Europe. The Fundamentalist controversy proves that vast areas of the United States are mentally twenty years behind western Europe.* Our universities do not function. Our common people do not read, because our books are too expensive.

He quotes Henry James, that very great artist and excellent psychologist—although only where the rich and cultivated are concerned—but that very silly old man when it came to his own country. That old man so divorced from his own country, so little understanding it, that he abandoned his citizenship when, for three years, his country

* How does Mr. Wells assess the present controversy in England over the revision of the prayer-book? In a world likely to be set afire at any moment, is this not devastatingly anachronistic? And the controversy is confined to the educated classes, whereas with us Fundamentalism is largely the interest of the ignorant.

refused to enter a war in which intrinsically it had no part. Henry James is describing a long journey from north to south. "He speaks of the general pretensions of the Pullman," says Mr. Wells: "The monstrous rumble of which seems forever to say to you: 'See what I'm making of all this; see what I'm making, what I'm making'; to which, in his character of returning native, he replies: 'I see what you are not making; oh, what you are ever so vividly not. And how can I help it if I am subject to that lucidity which appears never so welcome to you for its measure of truth as it ought to be?' "

Lucidity? Well, let us take the rhythms of the Flying Scotchman or the Paris-Monte Carlo Express and set verses to them. They, too, are pretentious trains. "See what I have made, see what I have made, see what I have made."

"I see what you have not made; oh, what you have ever so vividly not. And how can I help it if I am subject to that lucidity which appears never so welcome to you for its measure of truth as it ought to be? I see what you have not made, and what dreadful things you are making. I see hideous black towns, growing instead of disappearing. I see labor and capital farther away from each other than ever. I see you talking about and preparing for the next war. I see your middle classes vulgar, grasping, avaricious. I see numbers of your upper classes cynical and idle; learning nothing and forgetting nothing. I see your peasants in many instances no better housed and no more intelligent than your cows. And I see where, with beauty back of you, you are putting up a myriad of jerry-built houses and inane little villas.

"And I see, too, what you are making and have not made—you, the Paris-Monte Carlo Express. I see all the crooks and gamblers and prostitutes of Europe hurrying to the common meeting-ground which, to many Europeans, is the aim of all effort. Crooks and gamblers and prostitutes selling, the rich and the well-born buying. I see, oh, so vividly, what you have not made. And you have had a thousand years to make it in and we but a scant one hundred and fifty."

But Mr. Wells knows all this. He would agree with me about the Flying Scotchman and the Paris–Monte Carlo Express. It is only when he surveys America that, like most Europeans, he alters completely his perspective, his standards, and his classifications; throwing aside all logic, all discrimination, all knowledge of human nature, all the delicate connecting links that constitute analysis. Even "An American Tragedy" is not typical of all American bell-boys. I know a poet who was once a bell-boy. Undoubtedly some bell-boys ought to be hung, but by no means all.

And as to American slang—although I hesitate to say this in the presence of the shade of Henry James—it has at least coined one expressive phrase, to which I call Mr. Wells's attention. The phrase is: "So's your old man."

Let us get down to details. Just what does Mr. Wells mean when he says all Americans are grayish-faced, gray-clothed, slow-spoken? Just what does he mean when he speaks of our shocking publicity? Our secret lives? Our unintelligible lingo? Our sparseness of emotion? Our lack of religion; our ignorance of flowers, birds, minerals, natural things? Is he speaking of our fox-hunters, our polo-players, our farmers, our upper classes, who—the last—until recently, unfortunately, bought most of their clothes in England. When it comes to slow speaking, is he thinking of the drawling Southerner and Middle Westerner, or the New Englander, New Yorker, Pennsylvanian, and so on, who speak with the rapidity of the Elizabethan Englishman—a rapidity long ago lost by the Englishman who stayed at home.

Does he think every American—the whole one hundred and twenty million of them—gets into the newspapers and is brought up with that in mind? Is he unaware of the fact that, although the *Daily Mail* and its followers learned their tricks from America, England presented us with the tabloids? Doesn't he know that the man who made revivalism popular in America was an Englishman, Francis Asbury, and that revivalism is distinctly an Anglo-Saxon, or, still more, Celtic performance? Let him search the corners of Wales and the slums of Manchester today. Has he no knowledge of the actual workings of a democracy which enable fools frequently to seem in authority? Possibly an excellent thing, since experiments are tried and, when found wanting, cast aside. When he says we know nothing of birds, flowers, minerals, natural things, is he speaking of our poets, artists, foresters, scientists, the thousands of women who belong to garden clubs, the millions of Americans who have gardens, the millions of Americans who each year go camping, the sixty million or so rural Americans? Or, if Mr. Wells is not referring to these Americans, but— when Dickon Clissold speaks— is referring to the average American politician and publicity man, and—when he himself speaks—to the American gunman, American immigrant, the small-town religious hypocrite, the small-guage business man, the submerged city dweller, whom he must be speaking about, or at least, should be speaking about, since his textbooks are "Babbitt, "Elmer Gantry," and "An American Tragedy," what deductions are we supposed to draw? Would he have us suppose that the English politician is on the whole a charming and ingenuous fellow? That Austen Chamberlain has a mobile and expressive face? That Lloyd George is a symbol of neatness, smartness, and good taste? That the usual London clerk and city man is a ruddy, well-conditioned creature? That the English real-estate operator is a model of honesty and unselfishness? That Pecksniffs are unknown in England? That the English lift-man talks about flowers and birds and minerals in his leisure hours? That the English criminal reads Shelley to his victims while robbing them? That the newly arrived English Jew discusses philosophy? That Old Bill of "The Better 'Ole" is a gracious fellow fond of Austin Dobson?

When I was a youth I worked for a while in a university settlement house in Bethnal Green. I was told to teach baseball to a group of young East Londoners. It took me at least two weeks to begin to understand a single word they were saying. But it never occurred to me that all of England talked a debased lingo, or that "here was a people degenerating, worn halfway back to speechlessness and brutishness." Nor, when I came across Yorkshire peasants or Devonshire peasants whose entire vocabulary consisted of about five hundred words, did I think England was returning to the Stone Age. I remembered that after all the English were a race which had produced Shakespeare.

Cities foster grayish-faced men everywhere; everywhere the ordinary man is a child socially and intellectually, and sometimes a selfish and hypocritical child. *Noblesse oblige*—a rare and beautiful thing—simply means that somewhere in your family tree some one has acquired enough money or property to allow you and other descendants to cultivate the virtues.

I agree with Mr. Wells. In a general way—for I imagine that is what he means—cities are dreadful—that is, cities as they now are. There are no clean cities, no quiet cities, no cities that do not distort out of the semblance of humanity at least ninety per cent of their inhabitants—not even Paris, which is one of the largest forest preserves in the world. Most city people stop thinking after they reach the age of twenty; they function entirely by means of mechanical reactions. But there is one hundred per cent more chance that cities, as they now are, are a passing phase, than that ignorance, lack of poetry, lack of knowledge of natural things, is a passing phase among those classes of society, English or American, which have the least advantages.

Nor must it ever be overlooked that, paradoxical as it may seem, the very mechanical proficiency of America is partly due to the fact that no other country is closer to the frontier or to the soil. The American restlessness and the American passion for motor-cars are partly owing to this.

Englishmen, as I have said elsewhere, believe in dragons—that is, they fit the picture of the world to their own framing. No other race does this quite so expertly. I have an elderly English friend who is typically British. One reason why I enjoy him, but not a particular reason why I always understand him. One night, three years ago in France, he came to dine with us. On the table in the living-room was the latest copy of the Paris *Herald*, and on the lounge, just back of the table, were sitting two Frenchmen who spoke English as well as did my English guest and myself. But such little things as that have never stopped the English from expressing their opinions—one reason why they are powerful but not popular. At the moment, the Paris *Herald* was filled with the latest English divorce case, and if you know England, you know what that implies. A Mr. A was being sued by a Mrs. B, and involved, and intimately concerned in the most sordid and disgusting details, frankly given, were what seemed to be dozens of Mr. C's, D's, E's, and so on, and scores of Mesdames and Misses X, Y, Z's. So many of them that one English wit remarked: "That if this kept up, the cube roots of the alphabet would have to be used." Each nation has its favorite crimes and scandals, but for sheer unadulterated—one should say "adulterated"—strength it would be hard to beat an English divorce case.*

"Do you know," boomed my friend over the heads of the innocent French guests, and taking up a subject we had been discussing that afternoon—"do you know, I have come to the conclusion that what really separates us from the Latins—and when I say 'we' I include you Americans, of course—is our conception of the sacredness of the marriage vows?"

Exactly. So you see what I mean.

When I was at Oxford there was a great to-do—as there always is—about American professional coaching. It was doubtful if English university crews should row against American university crews because of this. The agitation was led by the coach of the Oxford 'varsity. I heard him make speeches on the subject. He was a don at Christ Church on a comfortable stipend, and he taught just one thing—rowing.

So again you see what I mean.

As a general rule, in any sort of discussion it is necessary to announce your premises and then limit your field of inquiry, or if you insist upon immense, vague, general pronunciamientos at

* The English papers are no longer allowed to publish details of suits for divorce; a suppression which, like most suppressions, has resulted in an increase of the evil itself.

least to admit of categories and the differences they imply. A man who stated that all horses had hairy fetlocks and large rumps would not be taken seriously in racing circles. But Mr. Wells cannot help himself. Usually a fairly logical man—exceptionally logical for an Anglo-Saxon—when it is a question of the United States he is not conscious of his lack of logic. He is played upon by a century and a half of tradition and prejudice. Even he is not strong enough to escape. He sees what he is expected to see; he believes what he is expected to believe. Better one bright remark about America, one sentence of brilliant summation, than a chapter of truth. Better and far easier to concentrate upon a Babbitt and an Elmer Gantry, than upon a Morgan or a James Hill, a Bishop Lawrence or a Cardinal Gibbons. Better to confine your attention to Main Street than allow it to wander to a Byrd who flew across the North Pole while in naval service, or to the Americans who, on soldiers' pay, offered themselves to be experimented upon in the fight against yellow fever.

As to American reading, the reading public of any country is shamefully small, the American reading public, considering our size, especially so; but Mr. Wells must not forget that most English writers make their living in America, and that it was America which discovered Meredith, Conrad, and himself, not to mention Galsworthy and, to a great extent, Bernard Shaw. Not long ago, Wells's "History of Mankind" shared honors as a best seller, if I am not mistaken, with Wasserman's "The World's Illusion." But laying this aside, again I would ask him, would he have us believe that the great mass of the English people read intelligently and well?

America is a continent. One should be a trifle humble in its presence, as the decent American is humble in the presence of the continent of Europe. To land in New York, or even to cross America, and then imagine you know it, is exactly like landing in Southampton and, after a month or so in England, writing articles about the Balkans. Much the same, for the most astonishing thing to the American who is aware of his country—and not many are—is the variety, despite a common language and standardization, which it exhibits. A variety so great that when you step across that arbitrary thing, a state line, you are in a different principality. Where can you discover people more unlike, for example, than those of North and South Carolina? Than those of New Mexico and Wyoming? But this variety is a delicate and subtle matter and not discernible to the casual spectator. Even our great cities are unlike; even our little towns; though the latter seem, on the surface, so much alike. It is a dull observer who would find the New England farmer similar to the rancher of the Rocky Mountains, the Southern cotton-planter the same man as the steelworker of Pennsylvania, the Chicagoan not to be distinguished from the New Yorker.

One becomes increasingly astonished at Mr. Wells and most of our other English critics—astonished and irritated; the latter despite a former denial of passion; for Mr. Wells and most of these critics are novelists, and novelists are supposed to be susceptible to fine shades of dissemblance and to deal in them. If any man has need of the scientific method of reasoning—that is, reasoning that moves from the often-repeated particular to the general—it is the novelist. Indeed, save when he talks of America, Mr. Wells uses this method invariably. If he wishes to paint a portrait of an American, he should do this—I present the method to all visiting Englishmen. Let him choose first a state, then a town, and in that town, a family, and then, in that family, an individual. After choosing the individual he should discover what strains are in his blood and what traditions. The Quaker of Philadelphia is not like the Huguenot of Charleston; the patroon of New York not in the least like the Puritan of the Ohio valley. If he wishes to be really a social commentator, he should then discover what especial stigmata this carefully selected individual carries. A large wart on the nose has changed the personality of many an American man or woman. A thousand such individuals, selected at random throughout the country, carefully studied, might in the end enable a foreigner to arrive at one dim, tentative, general opinion—provided, of course, that he had lived in America for thirty years.

Furthermore, even if you are in a position to form general opinions, there are two ways of looking at any country. The way you choose depends upon your temperament. If you believe all is for the worst, you disregard as much as you can the fine element of that country—invariably a small element—and concentrate upon the inevitable, under present-day conditions, large, gross element. And then you say to yourself: "This is what this country is coming to. These fine people do not count. Their fate is to become scarcer. Eventually they will be submerged by all this vulgarity and selfish stupidity. There are signs of this everywhere."

The other way to regard any country is to deprecate and condemn the large gross element and be sorry it exists, but at the same time to concentrate upon the small, fine element, which after all is the flowering of the nation. Is it decreasing or increasing? Mr. Wells thinks definitely it is increasing, except in America, where, as far as I can make out, he recognizes no fine, small element at all.

In all other ways a fundamental optimist, in this way only is he a fundamental pessimist—meaning by fundamental optimist a man who, however much he may dislike the present, believes good is on the increase, as opposed to a man who, however much he may enjoy the present, thinks evil will eventually win. Indeed, the fundamental optimist is at times a dreary fellow, as both Mr. Wells and myself frequently are; while the fundamental pessimist is frequently a cheery one, since fundamental pessimism is usually founded on a delight with yourself because of a vast contempt for others. That Mr. Wells should be pessimistic about America would indicate, therefore, that in this respect his conclusions are more the result of bias than reason. How otherwise, and using personal instances, could he think that all American statesmen look like Colonel House? We have, for example, a fox-hunting Wadsworth. How otherwise, with his own countless Utopias ending in conclusions "as trite as magazine articles," could he sneer at Woodrow Wilson for the same failing? Nor is it odd that he finds the American watchful and awkward in his presence. Nations are apt to be watchful and awkward in the presence of the English. Mr. Wells himself says that, due to the public schools and certain traditions, England has in the last hundred years produced a type utterly baffling to other nationalities and completely alien to what he calls "the natural Englishman."

Moreover, in speaking of Woodrow Wilson, Mr. Wells forgets. Possibly ex-President Wilson's mission would have been more successful had he, on the one side, been more tactful with his American enemies, and had Lloyd George and Monsieur Clemenceau, on the other, and far more important side, been a trifle more ingenuous. The news that Lloyd George and Monsieur Clemenceau, and all the rest of Europe, were regarding Woodrow Wilson as the innocent, idealistic, easily fooled schoolmaster that Mr. Wells announces him to be, reached America in a comparatively short time.

Most Europeans seem to have a genius for forgetting. Two summers ago the Continental edition of the *Daily Mail* ran for two weeks on its front pages two columns entitled, "Facing the Facts." The heading of these two columns was the simple word, "Usury"—the first two letters printed in extra large type, thus: "U. S." The principal point made was that England could not forgive

America for allowing England to fight America's battles for one solid year after America had declared war. In other words, that for one solid year America had landed practically no troops in France and had taken part in no large offensive. Outside of the fact that this is not true, unless one considers that a navy, and the material and military preparations for making war are not war, and outside of the fact that it also applies to a large extent to England's first year of war, there is an extremely sinister catch to it.* The ordinary citizen is allowed to forget, but the newspaperman is not supposed to forget. It is his business to remember.

All English newspapermen know that England offered us transport; all English newspapermen

* No one but a blackguard or an ignoramus would minimize for one moment the heroic history of the First British Expeditionary Force, and it is well to state here that that is not my intention. My intention is to point out to the English, and other nations, how extremely ugly in the American sight is the reverse process. Upon declaring war the British dispatched 70,000 officers and men to France; the French army had taken the field with 1,300,000 officers and men. At the first battle of the Marne there were 50,000 British effectives, as opposed to 1,000,000 French. In the autumn of 1914 the British held, out of 500 miles, 24. The first British action on any large scale was the first battle of the Somme, one year and eleven months after they had declared war; the first American action on a large scale was the Argonne, one year and six months after we had entered the war. At the end of the first year, dating from their respective declarations of war, Great Britain had 760,000 troops in France, the United States 380,000, but at the end of one year, three months, Great Britain had 950,000, and the United States 1,200,000, and at the end of one year and six months, the comparison was, Great Britain, 1,000,000 troops, the United States, 2,000,000. At the Armistice the Americans held 101 miles of front, the English 70. Once again, in giving these figures, it is not my intention to be invidious, merely to object justly to much of the talk now prevalent in Europe, and America as well.

know that this transport was not given until the breaking of the English Fifth army in the spring of 1918; and all English newspapermen know that because this transport was not given we took to building wooden and synthetic ships in quantities far exceeding their need as carriers of materials.

Subsequently Lord Rothemere dismissed incontinently the editor of the European *Daily Mail*, saying he had never been given the slightest authority to launch so vicious a campaign. Strange news to any ex-newspaperman. The English may have private lives, but at times they also have secret lives, lit by lurid flashes of publicity.

Neither is "America the creditor" an opportune phrase. To this the American can justly retort that "America the creditor" has been the most fortunate symbol English trade has picked up in many a year, and that English trade has not neglected its opportunities. When the war ended, America was the greatest country in the world, financially, politically, and commercially; to-day it is the greatest financially. It is well known that English statesmen are the most adroit there are; they have a history of adroitness. Beside them the French and the Americans are children. What could have been cleverer than to have come over here as the key nation and to have set a high limit to your capacity to pay, if afterward you dashed home and asked every other nation if they wished to deal with "the Shylock, the blood-money man across the seas"? I am not saying that this was the intention; I am merely saying that this was how things worked out. And I am merely saying that if the European nations wished America to forgive their debts, theirs was a poor way of going about it.

At all events, and however I may feel personally about the debt imbroglio—and I am not giving my private opinions here—I am exceedingly tired, in company with many other American citizens, of being held individually responsible. I have no doubt there are a great many Englishmen who object strenuously to the way King George creases his trousers; and I say this with due respect, for he is a fine man and I do not feel toward him as Mr. Wells does, but I do not believe these Englishmen can immediately change this condition short of revolution. By maintaining their position, by doing what little they can, in a hundred years or so something may happen, but not now.

This game becomes more and more fascinating and enthralling as you play it. England, for instance, was greatly exercised because of the words of Mayor Thompson of Chicago, who bravely dared King George to come to that exciting city and who, in England, is regarded as one of our handsomer and more refined statesmen. At all events, he is not thin and grayish-faced. But America, for some reason, refused to become excited over the speech, awhile ago, of Cyril Norwood, M.A., D.Litt., headmaster of Harrow School. Mayor Thompson hasn't quite as many degrees as Mr. Norwood, but his diction is considerably less tautological. On the other hand, Mr. Thompson is not so well-considered in America as Mr. Norwood is in England.

Mr. Norwood, addressing the eighty-second annual meeting of the London Central Y. M. C. A., Tottenham Court Road, W. C. 1, spoke as follows:

"The League of Nations is not perfect, and it has just suffered a bad setback. 'Abolish it,' cry the unthinking, 'for the Locarno spirit is dead and buried.' A bad thing for the world if that is true, for the Locarno spirit is the spirit of Christ. I ask you as Christian men not to abandon your support of the League of Nations because in the first years of its existence elements which are rotten have come to the front and stultified it. It may be monstrous—indeed, it is monstrous—that a country in the New World, far removed and by no means in the front rank, should negative the attempt of Europe to reach peace and settlement. It may seem to justify that bitter taunt of the saying that it may be that Europe will relapse into barbarism before America has had time to emerge from it."

Mr. Norwood in his first few sentences was speaking of Brazil—by no means an insignificant nation—but in his last sentence he must have included the United States, or else he has no sense of the English language. Furthermore, like most people who assume to speak for the Deity, he speaks for a deity who sees only one side of the question. God apparently has never crossed the Atlantic. Besides, one might inquire without exaggeration, just when Europe, or any other place for that matter, emerged, in the things that really count, from barbarism?

The "New Age Encyclopædia," published by Simpkin, Marshall, Hamilton, Kent & Co., Ltd., London, 1925, has, on page 122, volume nine, this generous bit of history:

"St. Mihiel. This was the first important action in the war undertaken by the American Army separately. Success was more cheaply attained than might otherwise have been the case, for the Germans were themselves on the point of evacuating the salient. By anticipating this move the Allies reaped an immediate and profitable victory. The forty-mile front was held by six weak German divisions—about fifty thousand men—with two divisions in reserve. Pershing's First American Army had six divisions and two in reserve, and as an American division includes thirty thousand troops, it will be seen that the attackers were in overwhelming force. But they had, besides, the assistance of French troops, together with heavy concentration of artillery and about a thousand tanks," and so on.

Strange how easily nations forget. In Notre Dame de Paris there is one of the most impressive tablets a man can find. It is of stone and it is emblazoned with the arms and the scarlet of Great Britain. It is small, and on it are the words: "To the memory of over a million men of the British Empire who lie buried in French soil." And yet last summer the French papers were filled with editorials in which, lumping Englishmen and Americans together, we were asked how we dared come to France with our money when we had given only in gold and France had given in flesh and blood?

Only in gold! When England, forgetting how France, in this way, talks about her, talks about us in a similar manner, I am amazed. I remember the four and a half million American soldiers who were raised in a year and a half of warfare. The one hundred and twenty-six thousand American dead—not a bad record for so short a time—and the men who died in camp or hospital died just as surely as the thirty-seven thousand or so who died in battle; the forty thousand Americans who enlisted in the Canadian army; the thousands of Americans still in hospitals; several friends who even now occasionally shriek in their sleep because they are wading in the blood of the Argonne; a whole generation of American boys pretty nearly ruined for the term of its life. And I remember how, even on this side, I saw the coffins piled ten deep from influenza and measles. Only in gold!

This is not sentimentality, merely decency.

The intelligent and fair-minded American does not exaggerate America's share of the war. He knows clearly the date of America's entry and what she did. He does not compare her effort to those nations who fought for four years. On the other hand, he does not like to have this effort, gigantic when it was set in motion, minimized. There was glory enough in the last war, and shame enough, for every one. All nations were brave, all nations were pitiful. It was a bloody and unsatisfactory business at best.

No, it does not do to call names or to make generalizations. The ignorant may be convinced, but not those who have been about. Let me, in conclusion, show Mr. Wells and his coadjutors just how some hypothetical American could describe

England—even a well-intentioned American; that is, if he wished to dwell solely on occasional English follies and vices and not on fundamental and prevalent English virtues. If he went to England, that is, determined to see only what was objectionable, sensational, and disheartening. This hypothetical American, like the average, by no means hypothetical, English visitor to the United States, would be saying nothing that was untrue and yet, on the other hand, nothing that was just. He would be speaking rather in the spirit of the Scotchman who, after damning everything French, added: "And that from a well-wisher, too." The description will sound strange to English ears, coming from American lips. I doubt if it has been done often enough.*

* I wish to make sure that all my readers know what the word hypothetical means. From certain letters received I have come to doubt how universal this knowledge is. Hypothetical, as I am using it, means, supposed, imaginary; assumed for the purposes of argument. No American in his right mind would accuse the English as a whole, or even as a small fraction, of the things of which my hypothetical American accuses them. Certainly not of not changing their underclothes, and yet there are Englishmen—a few—who should know better, who don't change their underclothing, for I have seen them, just as there are Americans given to the same carelessness. I am merely using this absurd example to show the absurdity of most international criticism. One wonders how it is that so many Englishmen, in other respects apparently normal, continue to see America—and other nations—as they do. Despite 1918, for example, they continue to see France as a nation of small, black, badly-built Latins, America as a nation of large, gangling braggarts. Not long ago I was on the same platform with a distinguished visiting Englishman who blandly told his exceedingly well-dressed, upper-class American audience that Americans were unclean, that their taxicabs and hotels were dirty and smelled, and that Americans were not only dishonest politically, but dishonest personally. Al-

Let us begin. I know England better than Mr. Wells knows America, although I can't be quite as sweeping as he or Aldous Huxley, since my mind works naturally in categories. I am bound to divide the English into classes. I can, however, speak fairly authoritatively in the person of the hypothetical American.

Very well, then. This hypothetical American despises the English upper classes. He thinks them the stupidest, most conventional, silliest, and least progressive upper classes he has ever met, and above all, the most inhuman; the vicious ones as conventional and inhuman in their vices as the good ones in their virtues. They are the only people he knows who delight in rudeness. But they

most exactly a hundred years ago the quaint mother of Anthony Trollope, in her book, "Domestic Manners of the Americans" said—minus the taxicabs—the same thing, and a pompous English naval gentleman, one Captain Basil Hall, when questioned as to what he considered the leading characteristic of the Americans, answered: "Sir, I consider it to be their lack of loyalty." I can see him doing it. If these accusations still hold good, if they ever did hold good, then, at least, we can be congratulated on the tenacity with which we have maintained our original racial types; in 1827 predominantly British, and the charge of mongrelism falls flat—that is to say, spiritually. If it were not such a serious matter, far too serious for nonsense, I would suggest that when the centennial anniversary of Mrs. Trollope's book, and that of Captain Hall's, arrives, an arch should be erected somewhere with, prominently displayed, the words: "To one hundred years of complete misunderstanding." Furthermore, to make the matter still more perplexing, it was not long after Mrs. Trollope and Captain Hall, and about the same time as Dickens and his "Martin Chuzzlewit" that two other English people, Thackeray, and Miss Martineau, came to America and liked it, contradicting by chapter and verse almost everything said by the others. Can it be that Thackeray and Miss Martineau, being better bred, were better able to discriminate than Mrs. Trollope, Captain Hall, and Charles Dickens?

are bullies, for if challenged, they wilt. He understands the Frenchman, the Italian, and the Spaniard; but he doesn't understand the Englishman, and no one else does. Nor does he care to. The Englishman is all in shadow save for flashes of vulgarity, snobbishness, cruelty, and meanness. He has no honesty about money and little honor about women. He is constantly subjected to a disintegrating publicity.

There are half a dozen periodicals devoted solely to describing his comings and goings and to printing photographs of him. He cannot eat a sandwich at a race meet without being snapshotted. My hypothetical American is tired of seeing him being married under an arch of swords and making one of a party formed for the purpose of shooting tame birds. Far from being frank—as he imagines himself to be—he seldom says what he means, and he is so hedged in by tradition and accepted standards that what he says means very little anyhow. His dialect is more sparse than any other human being, save the Eskimo, as Ernest Hemingway aptly remarks, and he has no metaphors whatsoever; simply slang phrases, horribly bent and flattened by excessive use. The lover wrung to ecstasy may say: "You're a decent little vixen." The phrase for all occasions seems to be "Rather!" And since we are going into things deeply, my hypothetical American adds that he particularly dislikes the way the English upper classes so seldom change their underclothes, when they wear any. He does not like the custom of playing a game all afternoon and then coming in and taking a bath and putting on again what you just took off.

In other words, English society, to the mind of this hypothetical American, seems a butlers' society—a society where a man is judged more by his clothes than by his mind or his manners or his grace. This American, for instance, knows of no other great city in the world, save London, where a decent man cannot enter any restaurant he wants after dark without evening clothes. In Paris or New York it is taken for granted that a gentleman wears evening clothes if he wants to, or if he hasn't them on, that there is some good reason for the lack; but the Englishman apparently does not know a gentleman unless he wears a white tie. Here then is a country run by tailors for tailors who have left off tailoring to become peers.

As to the English middle classes— But I will stop. My hypothetical American cannot think about the English middle classes lest he think too much of adenoidal teeth and a sickening familiarity; nor will he talk about the English lower classes lest a vision of the gray, sodden wastes of London and Manchester come up to him, and the sweet, sickish smell of gin. In fact, neither my hypothetical

American nor I will proceed further, for what we are both saying is absurd, insulting, impertinent, and libelous, even if the English visitor to America, when he describes the United States, does not know it. England has many sides to her, and most of them are magnificent. But there is no use approaching a certain type of Englishman with soft words. That type is born to dislike us. Very well then, they must at least be made to respect us. At all events, of one thing I am certain and will always be certain:

When it comes to deep going the English and Americans understand each other better than they understand any one else. On the surface the French and the Americans are happier in each other's company, because both nations appreciate the value of politeness, but in a crisis politeness is not what always counts. I have always been sure that if you lock an Englishman and an American up together where they can't get out, even an Englishman of the type of which I have been speaking, inside of a week, if they haven't killed each other, they will emerge fast friends.

And now we come to the real reasons why Mr. Wells and the rest of them fall into such gross errors, and one of these reasons is also the reason, referred to before, why, if any country develops a world mind, it will be America.

For one European who has visited America

there are a hundred Americans who have visited Europe; for one European who knows anything about America, there are a hundred Americans who know a great deal about Europe. To begin with, most Americans are Europeans comparatively recently transplanted. Mr. Wells cannot cut us off and make a separate race of monsters out of us. Even three hundred years is not enough to clear racial traditions and folk-ways out of a man's unconsciousness, and consciously there is not an American family of the educated or semieducated classes which does not bear in mind knowledge of its particular European descent, near or distant. But that is by no means all. American children are brought up on European classics, European fairy tales, European myths. All great European books are immediately translated into English and sold in America. American papers carry an immense amount of foreign news; European papers carry very little American news, and most of that, canards. Contrary to common opinion and despite the insularity and laziness of the average American, he is, none the less—whether he knows it or not—much more interested in Europe, and that in a more intelligent fashion, than is the European interested in him or his country. Every year about two hundred thousand Americans go to Europe who have never been there before.

On his part, the average European is interested in only one American thing, and that is American money. The eagerness of the lower classes to come to America has only one motive; the visits of the business classes have only one purpose; the conclusions of the upper classes are formed before they enter. America means gold to Europe and has meant that since the conquistadors of Cortés. Surely not a tactful way to approach any race; and if the European finds the American more and more inclined to speak only with his wealth, and that in a domineering fashion, he has only himself to blame, since he has taught the American that that is the way to make the European come to his call. The American is a little weary of trying to make the European love him for himself alone.

The average European does not read American books, except when, as in the case of "Elmer Gantry," "Babbitt," and "An American Tragedy," they flatter his preconceived notions. He does not read American newspapers or reviews; he does not buy American paintings; he knows nothing and cares less about the inner heart of America; and, most important of all, he seldom meets the American upon the basis on which he meets all other white races. To get along with the average Englishman, that is the Englishman of tory mind, and most Englishmen, spiritually, are tories, the American has either to fight, keep quiet, or else allow himself to be regarded as an exotic pet. English society is sprinkled with exotic American pets. They take the place of the dwarfs of the eighteenth century.

Europe stands in regard to America exactly in the position—not uncommon—of many parents toward their children. Old age has a tendency to become disinterested, to become even more egocentric than youth, to become cold and selfish. There are a good many old people who are aware of their offspring only for what that offspring can bring them. But that is never true of the offspring. Children invariably bear toward their parents a sentimental interest, no matter how inaptly expressed or apparently quiescent, or even, as often happens, emerging in the shape of hatred and rebellion.

At least half of the American population expects to go to Europe at one time or another, and when they go, spread out before them, in architecture, in art, in countless ways, is the soul of Europe from the beginning. Many, to be sure, fail to assimilate any of this, but the vast majority assimilates a great deal.

In short, the American, all save those of Oriental or African descent, is a European with something added, while the European can never be an American unless actually he becomes one. Perhaps this is the reason why certain Americans seem to me fundamentally older-souled than any Europeans. They have a certain shining benevolence, a rather beautiful humbleness never found in a European. I do not mean that there are not millions of loud and vulgar and unpleasant Americans. I am speaking of an especial, gently bred, or gentle-minded, type. And even those not so gently bred, or gentle-minded, are willing by the myriads to spend patient and humble years trying to learn all that England and France and Italy and Germany can give them.

Something very fine has come and is coming from this patience and humbleness. Meanwhile, many Americans can understand Europe; no European can understand America—not completely—not even Bertrand Russell.

The second reason why no foreigner can understand us—least of all an Englishman—is that at the very beginning all foreigners make concerning us a denial they make toward no other country—they deny us all semblance of class, using the word "class" in a sensible way. No wonder Mr. Wells is able to attack our universities because in "An American Tragedy," a bell-boy commits a murder. No doubt he imagines that Mr. Lowell of Harvard is merely a bell-boy gone good.*

Naturally, therefore, no description of America

* This is not as facetious as it seems. Follow Mr. Wells's reasoning.

is typical or realistic unless it is written in a language which the foreigner chooses to think is American and unless it describes people the like of whom he has never known before. Again, this is especially true of the Englishman, since his ancestors invented the English language and left it to him, apparently, in secret patent. An American book which is not exotic—and as a rule, vulgarly exotic—is not American, but merely an imitation of something European. It may have to do only with America; it may describe accurately the American scene, American characters, American psychology; it may have the mysterious and individual pulse of the United States in it; but none the less, it is an imitation. "Gentlemen Prefer Blondes," for instance, is American; "The Lost Lady" is not. Why not both? The American writer is in a predicament. Having been born to speak and write English, he is not supposed to do either.

I have before me a clipping from the London *Spectator*, headed "The Blatant Beast in America." Yes, you have guessed it. It is a review of "Elmer Gantry."

"The novelists of the United States are a distinguished company," writes the reviewer. "Some are still European in their souls and styles. A transatlantic birth has but given a new twist to their petals, a sharp flavor to their honey, something hybrid, even morbid, to their grace. Christopher Morley, Elinor Wylie, Joseph Hergesheimer, James Branch Cabell are varying examples. But another group—Sherwood Anderson, Theodore Dreiser, Sinclair Lewis, Ruth Suckow in her minor mode—have been developed from American conditions and are absorbed in American affairs."

In other words, if an American describes gentle people going about their comparatively well-bred ways in a country that after all is Anglo-Saxon by tradition, custom, speech, and law, if by no means by blood, he cannot be talking about Americans or thinking in American. But if he describes—and this is not said in disparagement of the writers involved, for they are doing a most important work—a lecherous scoundrel, a murderous bell-boy, a hypocritical business man, or a Middle-Westerner blackly drunk with sex, there, then, is the real America. The people who on the whole most decidedly run America—the American educated classes—do not count, for it is obvious that there cannot be any gentle people in America going about their comparatively well-bred ways since, in America, there are no gentle people—they all live in Europe.

Undoubtedly American life is fluid; undoubtedly the country was founded on the supposition that all men, as much as is humanly possible, should have an equal opportunity; but undoubtedly America, like every other nation in the world, is marked by all the perplexing differences of human society. Class is inescapable. It is inherent in human affairs. If three men were cast away upon a desert island, within six months there would be class. Men are not born equally gracious, equally brave, equally intelligent. Nor is there any nation in which the gracious, the brave, and the intelligent are not on the whole, despite the smallness of their numbers, the ruling element and the element to which all other elements, consciously or unconsciously, look up. Moreover, Mr. Wells, of all people, should know that there is no social or political theory intrinsically so aristocratic as the democratic one.

The third and final reason why, not this time the foreigner in general, but the Englishman solely, can never hope to understand America, is because the Englishman has always persisted and will continue to persist in his delusion that Americans are close to him in blood. We are not allowed a common speech or ideas in common, but we must share a common lineage. As a result, to all the other irritations involved, there is added the irritation a father invariably feels toward a self-willed son.

We are not English—only a small per cent of us. The English blood in America is filtered thin. But we are Celtic—a vast number of us. On the whole, we are a Celtic, or, in much smaller proportions, a Teutonic people, living, as said before, under Anglo-Saxon traditions, customs, speech, and laws. When Mr. Wells understands the Irish, the Scotch, the Welsh, the Germans, and the Scandinavians—something no Englishman has ever done —he may begin to understand us, but not until then. Understanding the Frenchman won't help him a bit, unless, among the French, he includes the Bretons. Even in his own land I doubt if the Cornishman likes Mr. Wells unreservedly. Mr. Wells is too Anglo-Saxon, too cocksure, too bland, even if his name has in it a trace of Cornwall.

I am reminded of what a Turk said to me a little while ago. I had been praising Kemal Pasha. He touched his chest and head, and said, "Thank you to God, sir. And now, if you will all leave us alone for a little while we will try to do something."

The Spanish are a wise race. For centuries they have lived in the midst of Europe, and for the past two hundred years they have not allowed this to bother them in the least. They travel about a great deal, they are always polite, smiling, good-humored; utterly Spanish and utterly self-contained. If the rest of Europe does not like them, that is Europe's fault. Occasionally they eat with their knives; they are not ashamed.

The greatest misfortune that ever befell America was when it came to be regarded as a phenomenon, a great experiment, a melting-pot—the last of which it was for only a short time, and now is prevented from being by law. If our visitors would simply regard us as a nation of one hundred and twenty millions, marked, as is every nation, by all strata of human class and intelligence, by all human virtues and vices and follies, a nation doing on the whole the best it can, whose one note of originality is the democratic bias, they would understand us better.

It is the European who is inhuman when he approaches America, not the American who is inhuman—unless outrageously approached.*

* In his answer to his American critics, I occupying an humble position in this retort, Mr. Wells accuses me of contradicting him simply by pointing out English faults, which is no argument at all. Mr. Wells also says when he plays tennis "he doesn't wear underclothes." Mr. Wells misses my point. I have already said my argument was not a *tu quoque* one, even if I did use the slang phrase, "so's your old man." The sole point of my argument was not to point out to Englishmen that they have faults equal to our own, but to point out to Englishmen that in all international criticism it is invariably necessary, unless you wish to do more harm than good, to say outright, "in criticizing you I do not imply we are any better." To say this, not merely to imply it. Always. Never to leave it out, even if, as in the case of Mr. Wells, the reading world knows his fierce criticism of his own race. The English, above all peoples, should avoid any trace of phariseeism—next to them, the Americans.

V

BEHOLDERS OF MOTES

V

BEHOLDERS OF MOTES

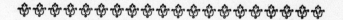

EUROPEANS have always charged Americans with being supersensitive to criticism. Let us see.

Personally I have never imagined that I could kick another human being without his resenting it; certainly not unless he was positive the kick was delivered in the most friendly and playful of spirits, and for the past fifteen years—that is, since I have achieved any sense at all—if I have felt myself called upon to give advice, I have first endeavored to convince the victim that my attitude was friendly. Otherwise I have refrained unless I wished to inflict or to receive punishment.

But that, after all, is not giving advice; it is issuing a challenge.

I do not and never will expect a kick prompted by contempt or anger to be received with affection, and I do not and never will expect a man to welcome smilingly my opinions if I preface them by calling him a hopeless fool. That, I think, is expecting too much. We are living in a frank age, which is good. Frankness is excellent, but it is well first to know what frankness is. Vociferous personal opinion is not in itself frankness. Frankness to be valid has to have about it a trace of universality, and it is so powerful and precious a thing that it should be handled only by the wise. At least those wise enough to know the difference between it and insult, and between it and prejudice. We do not put surgeons' knives into the hands of amateurs; the world will never be so frank that a man who clearly dislikes you can attempt with safety to describe you to your face. Nor can he, as a matter of fact, ever describe you accurately. Necessarily his point of view will be warped. It is a requisite of frankness that, to be just, it must arise from some degree of understanding and compound itself to some extent with sympathy.

Furthermore, there are certain well-established rules of criticism. That these are just at present out of fashion and that the recent release of man's ego has introduced temporarily a form of criticism, if it can be called that, which is entirely subjective does not in the least invalidate these rules in the minds of wise men. Nowadays a critic says what he likes, or doesn't like, and there, he imagines, it ends. But it doesn't, for that is not criticism.

All of which being very true and very simple

and generally recognized, I do not see why, as a member of a certain race or nation, my reactions or my demands should be greatly different from my reactions or demands as an individual. They may be broader and more elastic. Their edges may fade away more often than not into dilemmas difficult of choice. There may be much about my nation I do not like and about which I will readily admit my disapproval, I may find large sections of it beyond my control, but that is exactly the way I feel about my own small personality; and bad or good, that personality is all I have to work with, and it is a delicate mechanism with a pride of its own. Moreover, it is made up of many things, some of which I recognize as influences for which I am by no means responsible.

Back of it there is history, the mistakes and virtues of ancestors, legacies helpful and crippling, and it is subject to present environment and the painful necessity of curbing many of its most earnest desires in order that it may live at all with the desires of other men and be even part way effective. I can not wave my wishes like a conjurer's wand and have them miraculously fulfilled. For the most part I must work like a mole. If I am a wise man I will try to improve what I have; a slow, often blind, usually broken process, like the gathering together of odd bits of sticks and grass by a bird building a nest. Above all, I will try to appreciate and use the counsel of those whom I consider wise, but should such counsel be given angrily, invidiously or rhapsodically, I will reject it, knowing intuitively, and correctly, that it is not counsel at all but an attempt either to cheapen me or make me into something I am not.

In other words, I am I, with whatever faults and virtues I may possess, and in other words, a nation is a nation. And whatever you have to say about it, that, as the fundamental equation, the starting-point, is what you have to take into consideration. There is no use, for instance, telling the American nation not to be, on the whole, a nation of business men, because that is what it is, from necessity always has been and will, for hundreds of years, continue to be. It would be just as sensible to complain because the Florentine Republic was a republic of bankers, or that the Hanseatic League was a league of merchants.

If you wish to spend your time profitably, spend it trying to implant in these business men the aspiration to be the highest type of business man known—a fairly high type of human being—trying to make them, for their own profit and the betterment of their nation and the world in general, as broad-minded, as intelligent, as cultivated as business men can be. But do not complain or detest them because they are not hardy and thrifty peasants or princes of somewhat debatable princely blood. And do not forget that a business community can achieve a very high degree of civilization—a civilization in which the arts, philosophy, and the graces of life have frequently flourished better than anywhere else.

There is not much sense in a fox telling a bird not to build a nest—to dig a burrow instead. There is not much sense in insisting that a Jugo-Slav grow into a tall, light-haired, blue-eyed Norwegian like yourself. He can't. He is a Jugo-Slav. He can become a good Jugo-Slav or a bad Jugo-Slav. He may become an educated Jugo-Slav, in which case in many respects he will be more like an educated Norwegian than he is like an ignorant Jugo-Slav; but, educated or not, good or bad, he is still a Jugo-Slav, and both his vices and virtues will have to function within that physical, mental, and spiritual circle known as Jugo-Slavism, whatever that may be. It will take two generations at least of totally different influences and environment to effect much change, and meanwhile, if you cannot find any good whatsoever in the circle of Jugo-Slavism, or any hope of betterment within its wide, misty, shifting but at the same time unbreakable limits, you had better go away and concentrate your interests on something else. Your opinions will do you little good and humanity less. Simply to announce broadcast that you loathe Jugo-Slavs will endanger the comity of nations in direct proportion to the ability of Jugo-Slavs to resent your remarks. If you can find no good in the Jugo-Slavs, no prospects for their future, you had better seek the byways of some such study as heraldry, leaving amateur sociology alone.

Now I do not mean to imply for one moment that I think a commercial civilization, or any other form of civilization as yet evolved, the highest possible mould. I do not in the least object to Utopias, for they are almost always stimulating in detail and some day the makers of them may stumble upon something really useful, although, for myself, I do not think that is the way the world advances. I have no quarrel even with the philosopher who condemns the whole capitalistic system, although, once more, I think he will have to be made to confine his theories to the laboratory until they are workable—if ever they will be. I do not hold in abeyance the man who frankly prefers some other sort of system to our own. I merely say that to me his preference seems academic and that it is better to work with the materials you have. But I do object most forcibly to these men, or any critic, when, in putting forward their theories, they grant nothing, not even the invention or use of a fairly sensible makeshift, to those who disagree with them, and when they judge those who disagree with them, not by their failure to live up to the best that is in them, but by their failure to live up to something they cannot, at least for the present, be.

I am weary, as an American, of being judged by men—fellow countrymen or Europeans—who do not like America, who do not understand it, and who take no pains to find out what it is. Furthermore, I am weary of being judged not as an American and a human being, but as an American and not a human being—something I shall talk about later. In the meantime I can come to the gist of my argument and state frankly what I am talking about.

Rightly or wrongly, the average intelligent American feels that he has a quarrel with most European criticism, and especially with English criticism, because of all peoples the English should understand him best. Rightly or wrongly, he believes that he has always had this grievance and that recently, since the war, the grievance has increased in intensity. That the grievance is just, that it contains wounding and irritating features which distinguish it from the usual grievances which exist between all nations and that—most irritating feature of all—somehow or other, no matter how painstaking or amicable or patient he tries to be,

Europe will not listen comprehendingly to what he is trying to say. Europe will not listen at all. Europe will not even admit that he has a grievance, right or wrong, let alone trying with him to get to the bottom of it, to dig it up, to bring it up into the light.

Perhaps the American is all wrong about this. Perhaps he has become slightly neurasthenic nationally and imagines evil where there is none. But imagined evil frequently ends in results as unfortunate as actual evil, and it seems to me a wise thing, well worth doing, to talk this belief of his over with the American, amicably, rationally, and as if he were a human being. To permit a man to walk about with an unaired grievance is a dangerous proceeding.

Rightly or wrongly, the average intelligent American finds that European criticism about himself and his country falls, with very rare exceptions, into well-recognized categories, all of which invalidate immediately the criticism itself. In other words, that most European criticism where America is concerned breaks all the rules of sound criticism, most of the rules of good manners, and is, with a somewhat trying monotony, rudely subjective. It is not—to take a homely instance, but one which occurs to me, since I was recently the victim of it—sound criticism to remark, when first eating

Delaware shad, bought at some expense by your host, "Humph! It is a bony fish, not like the English sole." The Delaware shad is a bony fish and it is not like the English sole, but it has a flavor and fineness of its own, which make your personal disapproval a matter of idiosyncrasy. You are at perfect liberty to dislike Delaware shad, but you should not regard the fish as another instance of the benighted American point of view.

Rightly or wrongly, then, the average intelligent American believes these things, and he finds that the two main categories under which most European criticism falls are dislike and misunderstanding.

These overlap, of course, or rather, the latter is likely to be part of the former, though, on the other hand, there is naturally a considerable amount of well-meant criticism based on misunderstanding alone. Contained within these major categories are the following minor categories, to mention only a few of them: a complete failure to discriminate, where America is concerned, between what is best in the country and what is worst, and to assess the relative importance of the two; a complete failure to recognize that in America, as in every country, there is an educated and idealistic class with traditions, a future, and a power far beyond its numbers; a failure to understand the peculiar and intricate political and social life of America; a failure to realize that the America of to-day is not the America of yesterday or a hundred years ago; an avidity to seize upon all defamatory reports and overlook entirely any that may be encouraging; an eagerness to assign to America motives, intentions, and actions of which America itself is totally unaware; while accompanying all this, adding greatly to its poignancy, there is, coupled with the perpetual lack of good manners, in many cases a lack of gratitude for kindnesses received and an entire unwillingness to meet the American half-way. The intelligent Englishman, for example, when in France, usually will admit that the French have their own way of doing things, but seldom, while in America or out of America, is he willing to make the same generous admission.

The American claims that he is accused of crimes and stupidities he has not committed, or, being an intelligent American, that he is lumped together with his less intelligent countryman and condemned with them for absurdities that he detests, is combatting, and is quite sure that some day he will be able to cure. In short, that however wrong he may be about other countries, the European is at least inclined to take a bird's-eye view of them, whereas, with America alone, he takes a worm's-eye view; that is, he insists upon looking from the bottom up, instead of looking from the top down, and so never sees the top at all. And, above all, the American claims he is accused of vices, and berated for them, as if these vices were his sole possession and not world wide.

For a hundred years and more the Englishman, for example, has spoken much of American boastfulness. The phrase, "Yankee brag" has almost been admitted to the Oxford Dictionary. Yet boastfulness is a matter of class, not of nationality. The ignorant man everywhere, be he German, French, English, or American, is boastful; the intelligent man is not. Methods of boasting vary of course, but the essential fact remains. The Englishman, using his own especial technic, does not, as a rule, boast directly, he merely remarks upon the folly of everybody else. In the last war one rarely heard an Englishman say that the English army was the finest in the world. That was unnecessary. All you had to do—and this frequently—was to describe the utter futility of the others. The English critics of America in the early decades of the nineteenth century, Mrs. Trollope and her ilk, did not especially praise England, although in this respect they were not altogether backward, instead, by describing the horrors of America, particularly those of slavery, and omitting the equal horrors of

England, a comparative perfection was implied that any student of history knows did not exist.

A good many years ago one of the Arnolds arrived on a lecture tour, shedding "sweetness and light"—the Arnold's were always arriving on lecture tours shedding "sweetness and light"—and, delivering a lecture in Philadelphia, refused to begin before his honorarium of a thousand dollars was handed him. The lecture was under the auspices of the University of Pennsylvania, a fairly solvent and honorable body, but the chairman had not brought the check in his pocket, so there was considerable to-do and inconvenience to obtain it. It was obtained, however, and the lecture proceeded.

The subject of the lecture was the growing and regrettable materialism of the American.*

For some reason or other, due to our early history, I suppose,—the pronouncements of the fathers—Europeans have never admitted that we were actually a part of that division of animal life

* Here is another instance in point, indicative of the curious lack of logic Englishmen apply to American affairs. In an address entitled "Equality," delivered before the Royal Institution, Matthew Arnold, an earnest believer in equality, points to France as an example of the civilizing influences of equality and quotes the words of Menander, "Choose equality"; and those of George Sand, "The human ideal, as well as the social ideal, is to achieve equality." But in his other essays, such as the one on "Democracy," Arnold uses the very arguments with which he has praised France to damn the United States. Can such logical breaks occur save where there is prejudice? They cannot.

known as *homo sapiens*, but have always regarded us as laboratory specimens. And although you may be interested in laboratory specimens, you do not like them, and if by any chance they do not act exactly as you expect them to, you are very likely to execrate them. I agree that America is an experiment, like every other country, and a most interesting experiment, but I do not think that the molecules which compose it are in their entirety laboratory specimens. For my part, although possibly I am prejudiced, I have found them very much like men and women. Moreover, the scientific point of view, however excellent—indeed, the only excellent point of view—requires in those who would use it some training. The initial coolness of glance must be followed up by a subsequent coolness of discrimination. It is not enough for the European to approach the American with a coldly scientific eye, if the eye merely conceals passionate prejudices.

For the thoughtful American it is not difficult to see why all this is true; his difficulty lies in getting the European to see why it is true. Should he be able to obtain this result, he feels that at once half the misunderstanding between Europe and America would cease. At all events, he feels that it is of paramount importance to attempt repeated explanations under the assumption—perhaps an ingenuous one—that there may come a time when well-intentioned Europeans will discover what is at the back of his mind.

Between all nations, of course, there is constant misunderstanding, dislike, and inevitably the going up and down of the spectre of falsehood. The intelligent American realizes all this, and realizes also that at present he is in a position of dangerous prominence, and does not, I think, expect an exception to be made in his own case short of the millennium; but he feels, as I said before, that added to this ordinary misunderstanding, dislike, and falsehood are, where the European is concerned, extraordinary misunderstanding, dislike, and falsehood, due, as I said before, to extraordinarily wounding premises, and couched, as I have said before, and several times, in extraordinarily wounding terms. I do not think the American is wasting away for lack of being loved, and certainly he does not want any one to love him who cannot do so spontaneously; but he feels that if he could explain himself, most of the extraordinary element connected with the present dislike of him would disappear and every one could settle down to the nice, old-fashioned, and in comparison, comfortable, lies, misunderstandings, and hatreds common to mankind. The American would like to be rid of fifty per cent of the present point of view; he would be willing to put up with the remaining fifty per cent.

What this extraordinary fifty per cent is, why it is especially wounding and irritating, I shall have to put off until later, for there are other things to discuss first, and first among them is the persistent and vicious superstition to which I have already referred, that the American is peculiarly antagonistic to advice; a superstition working so automatically that the slightest protest on the part of the American against what he considers unfair advice is immediately regarded as evidence of this egregious failing. His case, in short, must be heard *in camera;* he is subject to Star Chamber methods.

Already, no doubt, many who have read so far will have called out, after the last paragraph in which I mentioned the average intelligent American's feeling that there are unique features to his charges: "How absurdly sensitive! How self-conscious! How puffed up with his own importance to think that Europe confers on him an especial dislike!" and there will be added, without doubt, that eminently handy, but as usually employed, meaningless phrase: "Inferiority complex." Well, outside of the fact that it is no evidence of an inferiority complex to reply, even heatedly, to a man who calls you, let us say, a worthless rascal, or something of the sort, there is enough evidence, growing in volume, to support the American in his contention. He is no longer to be put aside by gentle, well-meaning Frenchmen or Englishmen, outside of the current of events, who tell him that he is mistaken. There is too much on the other side—the European press, European books, the European individually. The American is not looking for affront; it is there.

There may have been a time when America, a young nation, was supersensitive; when there existed a real inferiority complex with its usual complements, braggadocio, unpleasant aggressiveness, a bristly search for trouble. Most young nations are that way, as most children are that way, and Europe, like an old-fashioned parent, seldom lost a chance to be disagreeable. Although, in all justice, it must be said that the little fellow, from the time of Andrew Jackson on, was frequently annoying; undoubtedly still is annoying. The more kindly European believed reproof was good for the little fellow—would make a man out of him. The less kindly objected to his growth and what it portended. Meanwhile, the little fellow was frequently having a rotten time, as most little fellows do, and was coming to the conclusion, as most little fellows also do, that whatever his character was to be he would have to do most of the making or breaking for himself. Parental sarcasm, kindly or otherwise, is, as a rule, merely hampering.

But it is absurd to imagine that the fairly full-grown, fairly intelligent, fairly sophisticated, eager-to-improve-himself American of to-day resents criticism if the criticism in its turn is intelligent and sophisticated. And the proof of what I am saying lies in that fact that European criticism which is just, understanding, and sympathetic, even when it is severe, even when it seems not altogether accurate, is never resented, and in the fact that everywhere in America are countless signs that Americans have been willing and are willing to learn from Europe. No one resents Rebecca West's remarks about America, sharp as they sometimes are, penetrating as they always are; no one resents what Santayana says, or André Siegfried, wrong as Siegfried's conclusions may be, or what Hugh Walpole says, or John Galsworthy, or Bertrand Russell, or Keyserling, and yet Keyserling exhibits the curious spectacle of a critic who does not like America, but who, none the less, is eminently fair to it, and strangely discerning.* No one objected to what Anthony Trollope, in contradiction to his

* Since writing this I have had to revise my opinion of Count Keyserling's wisdom on this subject. Returning to America after a long absence, and before touching America's shores, he has written several articles describing America to Americans that for sheer nonsense and pseudo-philosophical comment and prediction rank well with any of the absurdities in question. I was speaking of the Keyserling of "The Travel Diary of a Philosopher," not the cheese-eating, flapper-ogling lecturer of the present, who has so lost all sense of proportion that he calls his school The School of Wisdom. Milton once said that to be a poet one should live like a poet. I cannot imagine any one to whom a paraphrase of this statement would more apply than to a philosopher.

mother, had to say, or James Muirhead, or Bryce, or Arnold Bennett. When, however, a European pundit arises and announces that "without exception, wherever met with, the influence of America means the choice of the second best in place of the best, means a process of cheapening and vulgarization," the American takes a long breath and finds himself nationally and individually in a dilemma.

He cannot completely change himself even if he should so want; he is caught in the current of events; he cannot admit that he is from top to bottom wrong, even if he thinks so. He cannot go back, he must go forward as best he can. There is nothing left him then but to commit universal suicide in order to rid an otherwise charming, gracious, high-spirited, and generous world of his hateful influence—a remedy seldom resorted to by a group of men and women, and never by a nation as a whole.

Condemnation is not in reality criticism. The judge who is sentencing a man to be hanged can hardly be called a constructive critic, and to approach a stranger on the Brooklyn Bridge and say, "Look here! You're a dreadful fellow. There is nothing for you to do but jump off," may gratify your prejudices, but does not incline the stranger to a higher life.

A well-known British theatrical producer goes home and can hardly wait before disembarking to stutter his discovery that, in the theatre as in their homes, the minds of many New Yorkers work feverishly, but without a thought of investigation—in the theatre as in their homes, in the latter of which, drink, for example, is a complete obsession. This producer has met people who took tumblerfuls of cocktails in the middle of the morning, on the tennis court, and in the early hours at night clubs.

"What future," he asks, "is there for such a people?"

None. Every one will agree to that, even the people themselves. But why, when describing a few maniacs, use the indefinite article definitely? Why say "such a people," when you should say, "such people"?

I quote this as an instance of a well-known form of European comment; in fact, all my quotations are taken at random. One has no trouble finding material. But I wish to point out that I am not trying to make a single swallow into a summer. The sky is dark with them. For each quotation I use there are a myriad similar ones.

The New York stage is undoubtedly open to criticism, although—and this is not implying that two wrongs make a right—it is universally agreed by all but Englishmen, and even by many of them, that never in its history has the London stage fallen upon such a low estate as now. That, however, is not the point. The point is that the logical connections of the producer in question are frayed. One is forced to the conclusion that in his mixing up of people, cocktails, and the theatre he was not so much impelled by a desire to criticise the New York stage as by a desire to say something unpleasant about the American people as a whole. Not long ago a well-known English artist appeared at a dinner given for him by an American artist, a friend of both the English artist and myself, wearing a long red tie and announcing his arrival by fighting with the parlor maid who was trying to relieve him of his overcoat in the downstairs hall. Avoiding, however, the London producer's method of reasoning, I always imagined this to be an isolated case, or, at the worst, an example of a small clique, and it never led me to question the sobriety or good manners of the Royal Academy *en masse*.

The modern American does not object to criticism; indeed, if anything, too many intelligent Americans are too amenable to criticism, too docile, and unquestioning. We have probably the largest body of expatriates just at present of any civilized nation extant, which is not a sign that America is detestable and these expatriates intelligent, but that among the numerous sensitive-minded people we are producing, some are not very strong-witted. Expatriation—the kind I am talking about—is, moreover, always a sign of ferment and growth, like the curious and temporarily unpleasant complexions of the adolescent. Not that America is adolescent any longer; merely that the average expatriate hasn't caught up with it. Englishmen, looking back upon their history, can recall their own initial period of greatness—the Elizabethan. They will recall that Shakespeare spoke of "the Italianate Englishmen," and that in "As You Like It" occurs the following speech of Rosalind to Jaques:

> "Farewell, Monsieur Traveller: look you lisp and wear strange suits; disable all the benefits of your own country; be out of love with your nativity, and almost chide God for making you that countenance you are; or I will scarce think you have swam in a gondola."

The French have need to go back only to the time when half of France was engaged in fighting Jeanne d'Arc. The Germans have to go back to only a little while ago—just before 1914—when passionately but with odd results, they were wearing English clothes, a Continental edition of the English monocle, and holding five o'clock teas instead of their ancient kaffee-klatches. I think the last war made even more of a nation out of Germany than the war of 1870.

The modern American is not antagonistic to advice. There is no nation to-day indulging more in self-criticism, heart searching, and the pursuit of better ways of doing things. The cheeriness, which in reality was a reverse form of disillusionment, that immediately followed the war, and which hardly touched the more thoughful American, is dying away, and although the American is not likely to lose his fundamental optimism, he has become considerably more cynical. It is not criticism, European or otherwise, that the intelligent American objects to; it is the manner, method, and intent of most European criticism. And I am speaking of course—one has to make oneself so painfully clear—only of intelligent Americans, and I am aware that Europe, in her turn, has just as many complaints to make concerning America as America has to make concerning her.

Let her make them, and make them frankly, and good-humoredly, as I am trying to do.

The point I am trying to make is that in some ways, and most important ways, the American complaints differ from the European complaints, and that if this difference were eliminated—and it can be eliminated—Europe would still have enough legitimate complaints left to satisfy the most enthusiastic European.

I do not see why, in a discussion of this kind, the ignorant American should be considered anyway, except as a subject for improvement. Like ignorant persons everywhere, he is provincial, prejudiced, and unfair when he thinks about international questions at all, which is seldom. But he has not in such questions—indeed, he has in few questions—any real authority. As for the complaints, many of them reasonable, Europe has to make concerning America, they, too, have no place in this paper. To begin with, I am talking about the American point of view, not the European point of view, and to end with, for lack of space, I must leave these complaints to European critics. I do not think they will find Americans deaf to them; I do not think they have found Americans deaf to them, if they will follow, or when they have followed the simple rules I am trying to outline.

The American is a little bemused by this accession of hatred. Just before the last war he found himself rather well liked and the liking on the increase, and he does not know just what he has done to effect this change. He finds only two rational causes, one, the question of the debts, a question still open to discussion; two, his increase in power. But he cannot see what these have to do with his table manners, his accent, and his general appearance. Allowing for a slight increase in population, there were just as many unpleasant Americans before the war as there are now, and just as many nice ones. He is loath to put it all down to monetary considerations and jealousy, but he can find no other explanation, and so he becomes increasingly sardonic, bitter, and impervious.

I perceive, however, much hope in the younger generations, both European and American. On the whole, and for the time being at least, they have put war where it belongs, and in their social points of view they are different as well. The younger Europeans behave toward the younger Americans, and the other way about, quite as if they were rational and ordinary bipeds. In short, they treat one another—these younger generations—casually and naturally, in the way nations and men should treat one another.

Even, however, if some—even intelligent Americans—are still hypersensitive to criticism, I would not consider that an abnormal condition. Hypersensitiveness is largely an individual affliction and is about equal in all nations. The parable of the man who winced when the boot was applied to his own foot is older than America. All you have to do to discover the universal application of this parable is to fit a few boots. Not so long ago I wrote an article* in which I constructed a carica-

* See the paper immediately preceding this: "Furor Britannicus."

ture, a hypothetical American, who, deluding himself that he was doing the world good and that his intentions were of the best, described England as the usual Englishman describes America.

There was not a single thing this hypothetical American said about England that I myself have not seen or experienced, and there was not a single thing which was not a reverse of English criticism, yet the picture as a whole, of course, was grossly untrue. I repeated, and insisted, that the American was hypothetical, but my assertions did little good. I was deluged with English letters. Several eager sportsmen wanted to shoot me; an ex-cabinet minister, taking a sadly garbled press report and refusing original sources—my article—wrote a long and slightly insulting reply; there were editorials in the English papers; a scare head or two; a couple of parsons preached sermons. One correspondent wrote that he had requested the secretary of state for war to take diplomatic action, to which I not unnaturally replied that if our secretary of state took official cognizance of all that Englishmen said of America he would have little time for anything else; and another correspondent wrote a fiery letter in which he remarked that apparently I did not understand that an Englishman was a man "who didn't give a damn for any damn man who didn't give a damn for him." An odd way, it seemed to me, of impressing this point. Why take so much trouble to explain angrily your indifference?

I should hate to think the last statement true, anyway, and although I have often heard it, I have always considered it a racial delusion, due to the look of sang-froid required from that original Englishman, Jack the Giant Killer, when he heard what the giant was saying about him—a racial delusion hiding a sensitive and poetic racial soul. Meanwhile, before writing the article, while writing it, and after writing it, I was being very fond of England, and still am.

Somewhere in all international discussions a man should state in broad terms his attitude. It is seldom done, but it should always be done, and as for myself, my recent experience has made me wary. A single sentence will not do. Nothing is taken for granted, and to the obdurateness of words, their inevitable lack of decision, is added the obdurateness of the habitual patriot, always looking for offense where none is intended. With the fair-minded no explanation is needed; they will merely remember that to meet preconceived hostility it is frequently necessary to be meticulous. Even words of one syllable do not always suffice to make clear to the habitual patriot your harmless intentions. He is a good deal like the theatregoer to whom the librettist must first confide that he is going to tell a joke, then tell the joke, and then inform that the joke has been told.

Very well, let me proceed. And let me state first, as I have said elsewhere again and again, that I am one of those curious creatures to whom, in varying degrees, all nations and most of the people who compose them are fairly pleasing. I have lived in three great foreign countries—Germany, England, and France—and I have been in most others. Also I went to an English university. I have never seen a race that was completely repulsive or a country that was not in many ways admirable, nor have I found a country that had not something to teach others and, from others, much to learn. Furthermore, translating my opinions from international to individual questions, since nations are composed of individuals, I have never met a man or woman, save a cripple—and even a cripple has a transferred sense of physical completeness—who did not have two legs, two eyes, lungs, heart, and the usual set of reactions, however primitive. I have never myself come across an utterly uninteresting man—that is, one without interest to the observer, if only for a moment,—nor, on the other hand, an utterly wise one. Persistently, I find myself called upon in my own mind to condemn the folly, stupidity, and evil of circumstance; never, except as a labor-serving device, the folly, stupidity, and evil of the individual or mankind, save in one respect—and that is the individual's and mankind's laziness in not resenting and seeking to cure more energetically the folly, stupidity, and evil of circumstance. To think otherwise is to put the cart before the horse. Every one of us is a bouncing pea on a skillet much too large and hot for him.

In short, I have never found a race which, if I liked it, did not like me, and few men or women to whom the same did not apply. And whenever I have liked men and women I have never failed to find in them unexpected generosities, while, I have never disliked them without realizing that to some extent the limitations lay within myself and that by this very dislike I was preventing them from expanding even as well as they might. In other words, and to use slang, I was most obviously and seriously cramping their style. Undoubtedly this style in its flower would have been distasteful to me, since in its beginning it was distasteful, but had it been wise or necessary for me to have much to do with these people, clearly it would have been wise and necessary to meet them to some extent upon their own ground and to win to some extent their confidence.

By the same token, I have never known a race,

including my own, many of whose citizens I did not dislike, and I have never heard of a country which was not functioning far below its normal level and infinitely below its promise. Nor have I ever heard of a country that could be called civilized, nor one in which at least ninety per cent of its inhabitants were not still semi-barbaric; a condition which will exist, with no more than almost imperceptible improvement, for countless generations to come, and then only if the present status is not too drastically changed by war, pestilence, or revolution. As I see it, every nation is still a gathering together of savage tribes, recently nomadic; a fact not to become too depressed about, since, although humanity is many thousands of years old, only two thousand years ago most of our ancestors were running around clothed in skins.

I do not mean to imply that between nation and nation, and individual and individual, there are not great variations. There are, and it would be a dull world if there were not. The man who attempts to treat all men and all nationalities alike treats no one intelligently. Until recently American diplomacy and American missionaries have too often worked on this theory without success.

But the man who sees no differences, stupid as he is, is not half so stupid as the man who sees nothing but differences. The differences are the circumference of the circle, the similarities are its centre. The Japanese, for instance, does not mention his mother or his wife, but if you could find the key to the filial and conjugal code of the Japanese, undoubtedly you would find an affection for his wife and mother extremely similar to that of the Occidental.

The initial thing to do is to find the key.

The Englishman believes that through aloofness you can select your friends without further annoyance; the American believes that through a general cordiality you will make a large circle of acquaintances, from whom, by a process of sifting, you later select your friends. But friendship in America and England is identical. It is true that the Jugo-Slav must function within the physical, mental, and spiritual circle that is Jugo-Slavism, but that circle itself is contained within the broader circle of humanity, and at the heart of this circle, as I have said, sits always a common humanity.

You sniff a little? I don't blame you. This, you remark, sounds something like a service-club oration; at all events, it is the oldest kind of liberalism, repeated countless times. So it is, but seldom before in the history of the world has its repetition been so necessary. Each age has its own brand of sentimentality. This age has a curious one—a paradoxical, reverse sort of sentimentality. Liberalism for the time being has gone out of fashion. Indeed, America is about the only place where it still has any great power, and in America not among the ultramodern. In the search for truth and the disgust with ancient fables that won't work, there is a tendency to confuse realism with harshness, to make the ancient blunder of confusing sentiment with sentimentality, but in a way directly opposite from that of our immediate ancestors. They, not being able to distinguish between sentiment and sentimentality, did not know what sentiment was; we, in our anxiety to avoid sentimentality, are no better informed and usually manage, while avoiding sentimentality, to avoid that most necessary thing, sentiment as well. The results are identical. Meanwhile, I shall cling to liberalism as the only political mood I have yet seen that contains the slightest promise of progress.

Am I sufficiently definite? I hope so. I should like to make clear how much, personally, I admire all nations and how much, personally, I deprecate most of the things they do. I should like to make clear my eagerness for a real alliance of the civilized nations of the world for the purpose of maintaining peace, and especially my eagerness for a real alliance between those nations who speak the English tongue. But in the way there are difficulties and, unfortunately, but as always happens, the real difficulties are the small and apparently unimportant ones—the ones that most people think not worth talking about. To quarrel over the way a man uses a fork is a much more serious affair than to quarrel over the way a man does business. The English, for example, prefer to keep their forks firmly in one hand; the American, with what to other nations seems an unpleasant dexterity reminiscent of juggling, prefers to shift. Both methods have their advantages; neither is indicative of total degeneration.

I, for instance, am not enraptured with English manners on the whole toward foreigners or people of another class, nor the English social point of view—social in its large sense. I have never been enraptured with these, and I never expect to be, and I think because of them the Englishman is hampered wherever he goes. On the other hand, I have always been enraptured with English justice, English literature, the English countryside, and the heart of England. I do not like French meanness, French complacency, and French provincialism, but on the other hand, I have always liked, and will continue to like no matter what happens, French surface manners, the lucidity of the French mind, and the fine, gay, sad, hardy quality of the French.

In the mass of nonsense being spoken and written at present, occasionally a note of common sense is struck, and such notes were struck a little while ago by Ford Madox Ford and Frank Swinnerton, and in both cases these wise men dwelt upon the human aspect of international relationships, and the former emphasized the fact that war nowadays cannot be fought unless, by propaganda, lies, distortion, and bad manners, the peoples of the nations involved have been stirred up against one another. Nor can wars be fought otherwise, not in democracies, or countries, no matter what their forms of government, where democracy actually prevails. The latest school of history is inclined to dwell entirely on the materialistic basis of war. To a certain extent that is right. I have no doubt that raw materials, markets, colonies, and overpopulation are what the shell cases are made of, but the explosives they contain are the slow accumulation of years of myriad small incidents and malicious reports. And shells won't go off with nothing inside.

Distance does not always lend enchantment. The more abstract a thing becomes the greater its potentialities for danger; the more human it remains the more easily is it understood and controlled. President Wilson's mind worked with a brilliant humanity when, toward the end of the war, he insisted on believing, despite all propaganda to the contrary, that the German people were still human and, acting upon this theory, appealed to them over the heads of their rulers. President Wilson's mind became dishearteningly inhuman once it became involved in treaties and post-war conferences. Law is only vicious when it regards itself as a separate entity and not as the combined will of the people; a government runs head-on into error and seeks its own destruction when it falls into the hands of an inaccessible class; the horrors of war increase in proportion to the shooting range.

If you wish to test the last, ask an airman of the recent war about his exploits and, if he talks at all, you will be dumbfounded by the coolness and even gusto with which he describes dropping tons of bombs on regiments and towns. But if by chance in an air combat he saw the face of a falling adversary, that has always left upon him an impression of sorrow and distaste. He saw a man—a creature like himself—mortally stricken. Regiments and towns were too far off, too much abstractions, for him to realize that they, too, were merely men or, in the latter case, filled with men and women and children. If this idea in its full significance was universally in the minds of men, or rather, if universally the minds of men were capable of conceiving such an idea, wars would not even be contemplated, and international criticism would better itself.

Therefore, the man who first used the term, "the state," as something disassociated and aloof, as an idea and not a method of living—and Plato, although not the originator of this use, was exceedingly guilty—did the human race no good. Some day it will be considered treason against the progress of the world to speak of this country or that, as England, or France, or America, as if nations were abstractions and not congeries of human beings; to speak of any country, that is, without the qualifications that make generalizations decently warm-blooded. England is not England, at least not England in italics, France is not France, America is not America; they are all collections of men and women very much alike.

The American objects to most European criticism, especially English criticism, since the English should understand America best, because, as a rule, it seems to him either malicious or mistaken, or inhuman, or all three. But he objects to it particularly because in nine cases out of ten this maliciousness, this misunderstanding, this lack of humanity, arise from the peculiar point of view Europe reserves for America alone—and again England is the worst offender.

The American objects even to a great deal of friendly European criticism on the score that an outright and sober enemy is frequently less annoying than a funny friend. A good many young married people will know what I mean. A lover who is constantly finding fault, who is constantly trying to change you into something you are not, especially if he is amusing about it all, is likely to become unbearable.

The following quotation is exceedingly apt for my purposes. It is a quotation from a well-known English novelist—an English novelist who has often been in America and who likes it so well that she spends a great deal of her time here. As an example it is perfect in its tone, reasoning, and the impression it creates.

"Any American man, except a negro, can become President of the United States; and any American woman, by strict attention to business, can become the President's wife. But there is only one President, who, of course —America being a God-fearing, law-abiding country— has only one wife. Even the posts of bank presidents and corporation lawyers are too few to go round a population of a hundred million. So that, with all this gorgeous and free opportunity, there are more gloomy and discontented faces in America than anywhere else in the world.

"The great American ideal is that everybody should become something he is not. The great American tragedy is to remain what you are. Resulting from this theory of progress and happiness is the phenomenon of the American boot-strapper.

"Now, every one has heard of the American boot-legger. But the boot-strapper is an even greater national figure, just as the feat of 'lifting oneself by one's boot-straps' is an almost entirely American accomplishment. Obviously, if you really were born a plumber, and if the unwritten law of the land demands that as a real he-man you must die with at least a white collar round your neck, you have got to do something about it. You do. You lift yourself by your boot-straps.

"There are penalties, of course. I have met boot-strappers who were born grocer's assistants and have become millionaires. The poor things were quite hopeless. They had had to try so hard to be what they were not—smart, efficient business men—that their minds outside that one occupation were entirely atrophied. The woman boot-strapper reacts differently; she becomes nervous and over-wrought. Many of them develop acute ego mania, which is almost inevitable. For, if you really are not what you are—and women are more self-analytical than men and less easily self-deceived—you have to talk very loud and very hard about it in order to convince yourself. There are more ego maniacs—naturally nice, self-effacing people—in America than in any other country that I know of.

"There is this further disadvantage, speaking nationally, that there are more second-rate people in first-class positions than there ought to be. This is all right so long as there is plenty of room for the first-rate man who has no capacity for boot-strapping and so long as there is no sudden crisis. But I believe that an emergency such as befell England on August 4, 1914, would spell a series of disasters for America far worse than anything we know."

Now, to begin with, this lady bases her opinion upon a logical impossibility, also a physical one.

There is no such thing as lifting yourself by your boot-straps and it has never been done in the history of the world. A millionaire may be a terrible fellow, and frequently he is, but invariably—American, British, or French, or German—he has that curious quality that makes one man a millionaire and another man a general, and so, primarily, must be judged as a millionaire and nothing else. Secondly, second-rate men are in first-class positions in every country, and although in a democracy they may be more obvious and, in second-rate first-class positions there may be more of them, in first-rate first-class positions there are less of them. Competition in a democracy is fierce. America has had a number of second-rate congressmen, but she has had very few second-rate cabinet officers or presidents; America, being a democracy, usually begins a war badly, but she has never ended a war with second-rate commanding generals. A strictly non-military republic, she has produced three of the greatest generals in history, as I think every one will agree—Washington, Lee, and Grant—while there are several European countries which have not produced a first-class commanding officer since Waterloo. Thirdly, the lady has just enough truth in her analysis to make it doubly unfair.

Americans are "impossibilists," in which lies

most of their strength and much of their folly. That is, they believe, all things being equal, that a man can better himself, if not in his own generation, then in the careers of his children. This does lead to some temporary maladjustments, although to a steady mass improvement. But to say that the average American is unhappy because of this process is absurd and leaves out of account, if nothing more, the history of American labor and the life of the American mechanic. When a man is really unhappy he does something about it. The trouble with the average American is that he is too contented. Only the enlightened American is discontented, as the enlightened man has always been—and will be for some time to come—in every country throughout history.

Finally, the lady is amusing. Her attitude is that of an intelligent woman looking through the bars of a zoo. In most republics the president is debarred from having more than one wife—at least at a time. But this also applies to monarchies. And even Mustapha Kemal is going in for monogamy. The whole attitude of the article is bright and sparkling—what the American, with his deplorable use of the word, would call cute. One suspects that it is a *jeu d'esprit,* written, possibly, to buy a hat—a *jeu d'esprit* with, at the end of it, a hint of war. But you shouldn't indulge in *jeu d'esprits* about another nation, not even for the laudable purpose of buying something you want, if the *jeu d'esprits* are untrue, their intent unkind, and you are sufficiently well known to have your words quoted all over the nation you are talking about. And especially you shouldn't indulge in *jeu d'esprits* of this kind when you are addressing your countrymen, who, heaven knows, are, many of them, only too willing to believe fables, if they are unpleasant, about strangers. I am not describing the English in the latter part of my sentence. The failing is world-wide.

You see what the lady has done? She has accepted the hospitality of a nation, she had made money from it, and is making money from it, and then she has gone home, not with any intention of writing real criticism, severe or otherwise, not with any intention of trying to understand what, at least, is a large and interesting place, not with any intention of even being humorously kind as, let us say, Mark Twain almost invariably was, or Will Rogers is, but with the intention of being witty at America's expense. Now I should object to this as a man; therefore, why shouldn't I object to it as an American?

Here is another quotation, this time from a famous Englishman who recently has been devoting a spare moment here and there in his busy life to things American. He complains that he has received many indignant American letters. Well, he would, and half of them would be foolish. A good many cranks write to authors. The famous Englishman says that he has every intention to continue in his criticism of America, that he is interested in America, and would be a stupid Englishman if he weren't. That the world has grown smaller and that Main Street, America, is just as much his as High Street, England. And that High Street, England, is just as much the street of the intelligent American as Main Street, America. Good! So it is—or rather, so they are. No one could possibly object to that. In one paragraph he writes:

"The friendly European critics of the United States are impressed by the facts: First, that the elementary education of the American citizen is cheap and poor and does not fit him for his proper rôle in the world; next, that the methods of democracy used by the states are crude and ineffective and that they hamper the moral and intellectual development of what is still the greatest, most promising of human communities; and, thirdly and finally, that the American sense of justice is clumsy and confused."

Good again. This is real criticism and whether you agree or not, a wise man is speaking wisely. So far every one has been having an interesting time and has, perhaps, been learning something. But then the critic spoils his entire effect by a series of paragraphs of which the one below is an example. He is no longer a wise man speaking wisely, but an Englishman speaking foolishly. No further comment is needed, except to say that sarcasm is seldom a direct way to a man's heart, or even his brain, especially if he be a comparative stranger.

"I admit the immense superiority of Americans in most things. To mention only a few: They win hands down on films and flivvers, steel construction and advertisement, debt collection, and floral offerings, Bunker Hill, and bathrooms. American architecture is superb. Their novels are becoming more interesting than British novels, and London, I understand, is full of their plays. If no American writer can write anything to compare with the storm of Tomlinson's 'Gallions Reach,' yet Stephen Crane came nearest it in his 'Open Boat.' The variety of type in the American population as compared with the British is as 50 to 1. America invented flying. Oxford trousers again were a plagiarism from America. I could go on for quite a long time jotting down similar glorious points for Old Glory."

In the words of that famous dialogue, "The Two Black Crows," why bring all that in? In England there is an ancient custom—beginning, very significantly, about the time duels went out—called "pulling people's legs." It is not understood by other nations, or, at least, the "kidding" of the American and the "*blague*" of the Frenchman are totally different. The English should put an export duty on pulling legs. Humor, furthermore, with the English is almost entirely a class matter, confined to the upper classes and the Cockney; and the Englishman who belongs to the upper classes, or wishes to belong, suffers from the uneasy feeling that in order to show he is a gentleman he must always be slightly amusing. To the American or Frenchman who believes that humor has its hour and place, the result is invariably baffling when not wearisome.

I have been throughout completely humanistic in my point of view because I believe that is the only intelligent point of view, particularly in international questions. Important as battle-ships are, they are not one-half so important as editorials and personal contacts, and so when I come to my concluding argument, the core of all my arguments, —the reason why Europe, and especially England, continues to misunderstand America and why America finds this misunderstanding more than ordinarily irritating—what I have to say will be so human that to many people it will seem absurd. I only wish it were.

Primarily and fundamentally the American objects to most European criticism because the European assumes that he is the criterion of manners, beauty, idealism, intelligence, and methods of living, whereas the intelligent American, by observation, reading, and acquaintanceship is bitterly aware that this is not so. It is not that he thinks he knows much about such matters, he is merely aware that the European is little better off, and that if anything is to be done it can only be started by a trifle more emphasis on universal humility. In this conclusion he is upheld by all the wiser minds of Europe. These wiser minds, humble about themselves, only cease to be humble when they survey America.

The American, for instance, finds it illogical when the Frenchman accuses him of materialism, the Englishman of hypocrisy, the East Indian of childishness. He does not see about him elsewhere in the world any great store of altruism, honesty, or maturity. And he cannot see how the minute store in existence can be added to if the European continues to castigate the United States for the folly, ignorance, and bad manners held in common. Once a European arises—in the past they did arise from time to time, but nowadays we are too rich to be observed clearly save by a genius of fair-mindedness—once a European arises who will say, "See here, you don't amount to much, and I'm going to tell you about it, but do not misunderstand me, we don't amount to much, either," the streets of America will bloom with the flags of that European's country. But this is a difficult thing for a European to do.

Having emerged from what was almost complete barbarism only about four hundred years ago, Europe, aided by the decay of ancient civilizations —a decay coincident with Europe's emergence—was able to impose its will in most respects upon the world. That is a bad thing. The only way a parvenu ever really learns is by comparing himself with some one whom he fears and admires. Europe has never had such an opportunity—at least, not since the Crusades, when the germ of European manners was acquired. Now, it is a characteristic of ancient civilizations, as it is of well-bred people, to leave, as much as possible, other nations and people alone—a characteristic exhibited by the Chinese until recently; to leave them alone, that is, while at the same time studying them and, if necessary, learning from them. Certain European nations are older than others and therefore more tolerant, but the newest of all—that is, the latest to emerge into world power with the exception of Germany, now temporarily in abeyance—was England. If you add to this fact great courage and a native Anglo-Saxon tendency to interfere and reform, plus Calvinistic teaching in that direction, you have what is frequently an unfortunate combination. This is intensified when the victims of it, for their sins, speak the English tongue and so can be treated as colonials or provincials.

These colonials and provincials are undoubtedly, springing from a semibarbarous stock, semibarbarous themselves, but they have this advantage: Not being completely sure of themselves, they can at least compare themselves with Europe and learn what to do and what not to do. Their growth has not stopped.

For two hundred years or more, since he himself emerged from the self-consciousness and social insecurity that followed the expansion of the Elizabethan period, the Englishman has occasionally admitted, where other nations were concerned, political equality, but never spiritual or social equality. Having captured the summit by extraordinary adroitness and commercial and naval success, he has sat there calmly, dictating his whims to the rest of humanity. If his mood was to be uncouth, then uncouthness everywhere was the sign of a gentleman. Regard, for instance, the reign of George the IVth. If his mood was to be brutal—and unfortunately too often it has been—then brutality was the mark of the aristocrat. For two hundred years, and at least three-fourths of the time when he wasn't, the Englishman has assumed that he was the gentleman par excellence of the world. As Milton said: "When God wanted anything very difficult done he called upon an Englishman." Yes —occasionally. Also, occasionally, when he wanted something very beautiful done; also—occasionally —when he wanted something very dreadful done. The record, on the whole has been about that of every other nation. It has been very bad for the Englishman to think otherwise. The reason he began to think otherwise was because in the beginning he was such a small, remote, shivering sort of fellow, and too suddenly great good-fortune came to him. No wonder he dislikes other nations and is unable to understand them.

The Englishman has never been able quite to tell the Frenchman that he was a barbarian, but he has told most other nations they were, and if by chance any of the nations happened to be a colony or an ex-colony, full use has been made of the added opportunities. If you were a German, that, being such an outlandish fact, to some extent excused you, but if you were of English blood or in the English tradition no mercy was to be expected. It made no difference that distance and environment, and peculiar difficulties caused you to produce variations of your own; these variations were not worthy of dignified criticism. The list of Englishmen who have paid America the primary compliment of scholarly attention is small—Bryce, Trevelyan, a few others.

The subtle and baffling feature of all this is that, although most Englishmen are possessed of these characteristics, few Englishmen, no matter how liberal, or fair-minded, or progressive, have as yet reached the point of perception where they recognize the characteristics in themselves. An Englishman may recognize them in other Englishmen, and dislike these Englishmen accordingly and rail against them, but when it comes to himself he is unaware of the permeation in his own personality. For instance, the woman novelist I have already quoted said not so long ago, and in curious contradiction to her latest statement, that she preferred to live in America because people were not so continually hating one another. Those who like the English learn to forgive these characteristics; those who do not like them—and that, unfortunately, is most of the world—find their hands strengthened. I can think of no simile except the vulgar one of halitosis, in which the sufferer is unaware of something about which most of his friends refuse to tell him.

At all events, good or bad, signs of an innate frankness and honesty, or of innate selfishness and obtuseness, these characteristics are anachronistic. They cannot survive much longer into this century.

Main Street and High Street are indeed next-door neighbors. Again, I find much hope in the younger generation.

But not only have these English characteristics been intensified where America is concerned; they have had, to increase their sharpness, two added features: America is an English-speaking nation in the Anglo-Saxon tradition, and will always remain so—or at least until some cataclysm happens—despite the pessimistic predictions of overly imaginative prophets such as Lothrop Stoddard, or even of historians as wise as Hendrik Van Loon. Whatever its blood is or will become, and the alien quality of that blood is greatly exaggerated, America's governing classes will continue to speak, without much dialect, the English tongue, and to accept—with modifications—the English traditions.

Therefore, on the whole, no matter what their ancestry—with two notable exceptions, and the hostility of these exceptions will disappear in time—the governing classes of America will continue to have, what they have always had, an instinctive sympathy with England.

But this must be distinctly remembered: The American no longer thinks of his speech or his traditions as being exclusively English. He regards the speech as much his own as any one else's, and the traditions, with their modifications, also as much his property as they are the property of others. In short, he is an American and nothing else. None the less, the majority of intelligent Americans want to like England, whether they are conscious of this desire or not, but as a rule they do not get the chance. England can take that, or leave it, as she sees fit.

Secondly, and here is a most important point, a most wounding feature—the most wounding feature, possibly, of all, and one never to be overlooked—while most antagonistic criticism and certainly all maliciously antagonistic criticism of England, or Europe, in America is confined to the ignorant or certain racial minorities who have hostile traditions, English or European criticism of America comes from what should be the most intelligent and broad-minded class in England, or on the Continent. It is easy to dismiss the words of a narrow-minded man; it is difficult to dismiss the words of a supposedly broad-minded one. The answer to this riddle is that where America is concerned, most intelligent and broad-minded Englishmen, most intelligent and broad-minded Europeans, cease to be one or the other, although their words, coming from men, as I have already said, intelligent and broad-minded in other respects, carry a weight they do not deserve—a weight and a poison.

The worst classes in America criticize Europe;

the best classes in Europe criticize America. There is an obvious retort to this statement, but the American does not believe it to be a fair one for, with all his faults, he believes that he is sufficiently civilized and interesting to deserve at least some sympathy from the better minds of Europe.

In short, here is the way the minds of even the fairest European critics work. They do not, as does the average critic, deny us all idealism, all good manners, all achievement of an imaginative sort. They admit we have certain classes given more or less to these things, but they proceed to the further statement that, in America, such classes do not count and cannot count. If such classes do not and cannot count in America, how can they count anywhere else? In any nation their numbers are small. And if they do not count, and cannot count in America, how is it that they have existed all through American history and that they are increasing instead of decreasing? Human beings are not given to making hopeless martyrs of themselves in such a fashion. If what the average European critic has been saying ever since 1776 is true, there would not be a single idealist, a single actual artist, a single altruist left in America to-day.

Here, in my hand, is a typical English letter, written by what seems a fairly intelligent, fairly pleasant Englishman. He states gracefully that there are numerous excellent people in America. "More charming, liberal, and interesting people one cannot find in the world"; but, "it is the mass of the people that gives the prevailing tone to a country."

Indeed? If this is so, then the prevailing tone of Athens was that of slaves, of China, in its greatest period, that of coolies; and what, may I ask, is the prevailing tone of England to-day? Or the prevailing tone of England in history? The answer, of course, is that my correspondent has put into words as lucid and simple a statement of an historical error as can well be imagined.

In a recent foreign commentary on the United States, there is this, quoted from an English weekly, although Canada in this instance is referred to, not the United States:

"To be sure, all 'nice' people favour English connection. They come to England every year and have many friends here. Some of them even bear English titles. But in democracies it is not the nice but the nasty people who govern."

In other words, it was "the nasty people" who dictated all the policy of Rome, of Greece, of Florence, of Venice; and it is "the nasty people" who dictate all the policy of modern France, of Switzerland, of the entire list of South American republics. Indeed, there is practically no place left where "nice people" have anything to do with what is going on save in England. But whereas, in these other countries, "the nice people," although they may be politically impotent, are powerful in other respects, in America it is as if they were non-existent.

It is this sort of criticism to which the American objects, and rightly, for it is without head or tail, rhyme or reason. It shows, to begin with, that the critic postulates that he is an authority on "nice people," a postulation frequently contradicted by his personal manners; and it affirms, in the second place, the American's conviction that his country is the favorite exercise-ground for European ill-temper, uncouthness, and prejudice. These are only a few of the prepensities such criticism exhibits.

Let us take at random another example.

American illiteracy has become a favorite talking point with our foreign critics, also with the majority of American observers, and it is indeed mortifying to discover that America, with all her wealth and power, is tenth on the list of nations with a percentage of 6.0. It is still mortifying, but not quite so poignant, when one sees that England and France are tied for the next place with percentages of 1.8, or, one might say justly, 2.0. In other words, for every illiterate in France or England, there are three in the United States. But the population of America is three times that of England and almost three times that of France, and the area of America is 3,026,789 square miles, that of France, 212,659 square miles, and that of England, 50,874 square miles. The mere administration of such a vast territory is a prodigious task. This vast territory is subject to all manner of climatic conditions. Any one who has seen school children in our far Western States, riding through snowstorms that are almost blizzards, to a school three or four miles away does not wonder that illiteracy in the United States is a difficult problem to solve. Until recently America was not an especially rich country and was engaged in the strenuous occupation of settlement. Until recently France and England were enormously rich countries and, with small territories, dense populations, and good communication, had both enjoyed over a century of peace, if one excepts a few small foreign wars on the part of England and the brief interlude of the Franco-Prussian War. Yet the best England and France could do, under practically perfect conditions, was only two-thirds better than what, under most difficult conditions, we were able to accomplish. I do not think that either Frenchmen or Englishmen should dwell too much on these statistics.

As a matter of fact, illiteracy is largely a question of size and population if we except Germany, whose percentage is the remarkable one of .2. The other leading countries in this respect are Denmark, Switzerland, Norway, the Netherlands, and so on. No doubt if a large share of the energy and wealth of America was poured into Rhode Island it would be a very perfect province.

I do not believe the average well-intentioned Englishman—let us confine ourselves once more to the Englishman—is as aware of all this as he thinks himself to be. I doubt if he realizes the flood of abuse, misunderstanding and even insult, that has been poured upon America's head since the war—a flood that is growing instead of receding. I doubt if he knows the long history of the English visitor to America—the history of celebrities, of ordinary travellers. It is a gruesome history. The American knows, and he has been a fool to accept this history, and sit silent under it. Why, with his peculiar point of view, shouldn't the Englishman treat him as a conquered provincial so long as he is willing to accept that treatment? The average well-intentioned Englishman is sitting at the small end of a funnel where America is concerned.

For example, he reads as a rule only one newspaper; he hears, therefore, all the stupid things that America says and the carefully selected list of horrors America has committed. He does not know the stupid things his own country is saying, or the horrors it is committing, and even sometimes, when he sees the latter, he does not recognize them as such. This, of course, applies to the American as well where England is concerned. The English writing man, however, and the American writing man by the very nature of their jobs are much better informed.

I take it, of course, that I am addressing well-intentioned people, both English and American. There is not much use addressing any others. And I take it that the well-intentioned Englishman and American—one could almost say, every sensible Englishman and American—regard as the ultimate misfortune that could befall the world any serious misunderstanding between England and America.

VI

THE REST OF THE BABBITTS

VI

THE REST OF THE BABBITTS

IT is not generally known, but the Babbitt family was and is, for it is composed of healthy folk who do not die easily, much larger than one was led to suppose from the distinguished novel the hero of which was the eldest boy, George. Moreover, like most prosperous and virile middle-class stock, this virility, as the boys and girls grew to young manhood and womanhood, has expressed itself in amazingly varied ways, ways so various that they would seem incompatible in the same blood were it not for a fundamental likeness. But then this, of course, is a phenomenon frequently witnessed in American life. One of the best ways to produce an artist or a rebel, although not perhaps the best way to produce a supreme artist, is to give him or her several generations of repression and a relative or so to despise.

This was what happened to the Babbitts, and for a while it looked as if some of them might be real artists and real rebels, if not supreme ones. But this hope is fast disappearing. No real artist "runs things out," to use an old undergraduate phrase, and the real rebel or revolutionist is so busy changing his mind and bettering his opinions to keep up with the changing world around him that nobody knows, especially himself, just what he is. At all events, he is seldom tiresome.

It is, however, a trait of the Babbitts to "run things out," and it is another trait of theirs to appropriate to themselves labels. George F., as we all know, went into real estate. Other brothers and sisters departed for New York, where they began to spell their ordinary names somewhat pedantically and to write book reviews, and novels, and verse, and meet once a week or so to assure themselves, not in words but by their auras and by steam heat, that they were the last word in revolt, intellectual freedom, and a magnificent realism. Always a sentimental attitude, to be sure; but we will let that pass. There is no need to busy ourselves with the lesser artistic Babbitts, any more than there is need to busy ourselves with the remaining children who, following the lead of George F., became lesser business Babbitts.

The world is passing them by. They are somewhat in the position of motion-picture magnates who decide on Monday what the people want, only to find on Tuesday it isn't so. There is nothing more pathetic than a group of rebels whose rebellion has moved on, leaving them unaware of the progress. A wrecked town after a cyclone is gay compared to it.

George F., the so-called, but wrongly, conservative, epitomizes one side of the picture; his New York brothers and sisters, the so-called, but wrongly, progressives, epitomize the other, so they will do for our purposes; the point being that George and his metropolitan brothers are all Babbitts, a truth that is becoming more and more discernible. Babbitts are born not made. Once a Babbitt always a Babbitt.

With which we can leave the Babbitts for a while and turn to a necessary attempt to redefine certain words and certain mental attitudes; invariably, of course, one way of running head on into trouble.

Words are treacherous enough as it is—even the simplest of words. No sooner are they invented than they take to themselves new shapes and colors. They are as absorbent as a sponge and as expansive as a drop of water. It is safe to say that ninety per cent of the world is born and dies never having said more than a dozen sentences that expressed exactly what was intended. Words, as I say, are treacherous enough as it is, but when mankind, with its passion for the concrete and for categories, steals an abstract word and applies it to concrete and particular instances, confusion is thrice confounded.

Examples of this can be multiplied, but in America we need search no further than the example America has made classic. An example, curious and sardonic, laughable, if it were not potentially so hazardous. I refer to our use of the words democrat and republican. In 1828 we chose the first as the label for a political party, in 1854 we chose the second as the label for a party in opposition, and ever since, for ten decades in the former instance and seven in the latter, the actual meanings of these terms have been largely lost to the American consciousness. Meantime, they have become entangled with half a hundred concepts having nothing whatsoever to do with the original and valid definitions. Concepts, to mention only a few of them, such as states' rights, a strong central government, slavery, abolition, free trade, and protective tariffs. Connotations having no inherent connection with the word democrat, which comes from two Greek words, *demos*—people—and *krateo*—rule—meaning, therefore, a believer in the rule of the whole people; or republican, which comes from two Latin words, *res*—affairs—and *publica*—public—and which by no means implies the same thing.

Think that over for a few moments and you will realize the power and danger of words. The greatest republic in existence, the chief protagonist of democracy, inhabited by a race the vast majority of which has no idea what republican or democrat really mean. While in Europe—essentially undemocratic Europe—a Europe not bemused by debased usage save in a few spots such as Russia and Germany where the word democrat, at least, has been almost as much mishandled as with us, there is no similar ignorance. Almost any intelligent Englishman can tell you precisely what a republican or a democrat is. All the centuries of careful distinction, and experiment, and experience gone largely for nothing so far as the people most interested are concerned. If you lose out of your consciousness a correct definition, you lose a concept, for there are in English no perfect synonyms. If you do not know what democrat and republican really mean, do not know as the founders of America knew, then, if your number is increasing, the country you live in is in danger of becoming neither a democracy nor a republic. And that, of course, is exactly America's present danger.

Do you think that is too fine drawn? I congratulate you on your optimism.

But if the comparatively simple words democrat and republican have been abused, what of such difficult words as progress and reaction, and what especially of that most difficult word of all, the supposedly red word revolution? A word that has been compressed or expanded to suit every need and all occasions, that has been twisted and bent to fit a myriad temporary and short-sighted purposes of mankind, that has been used as a bogy to frighten children, and as a cloak to cover the most varied forms of disingenuousness or stupidity. A word that has been borne as a shield by millions of charlatans and tied as a blindfold by the selfish and tyrannical; which has been hurled by every social coward and miser of life at the heads of the adventurous and open-minded, just as the other abused word, reactionary, is hurled by the pseudo-revolutionist at the heads of all those who do not completely agree with him.

You cannot talk about the Babbitts without defining reaction and revolution, because half of the family considers itself conservative, and therefore sanely reactionary, and the other half considers itself progressive, and therefore healthily revolutionary. In fact, that's where all the trouble began.

All through history the Babbitts have been hurling these terms at one another's heads, while what progress the world has made, slow and stumbling, has been the work for the most part of men too busy to call names.

Revolution isn't a red word, except when men, almost invariably for adequate reasons, have been forced to take up arms. No revolution ever in history has succeeded save when there was a crying need for it. Three-fourths of all revolution has been peaceable and unrecognized as such. Revolution is a good, round, solid, wholesome word, standing for all human progress. So surely it is not a waste of time to try to restore it somewhat to its proper meaning and to the delicate and discriminating values attached to that meaning, if for no other purpose than to take it out of the hands of the pseudo-revolutionists who nowadays have appropriated it. At all events, until we make some such discrimination, progress—in this country particularly, for we are given to catch phrases and shibboleths—will be hampered and constantly misunderstood, and the pseudo-revolutionist will exert an influence he does not deserve. Moreover, as said before, you can not otherwise analyze the position of the left wing, the pseudo-revolutionary wing, of Babbittry. Young people will continue to regard its members as prophets, older people will continue to regard them as dangerous, when, really, they are neither dangerous nor prophetical, merely Babbitts very much preoccupied with their own aggrandizement.

Let us begin by considering the actual definition

of the word revolution. The philologist has an advantage over most of us in this respect, for he is constantly checking up present-day and casual usage with original significations, and so gains historical perspective. Revolution, then, means just one thing, to revolve. It comes—to be etymological for the third time—from two Latin words, *re* —back—and *volvo*—turn or roll—and obviously, when first applied to the processes of the human mind, was figurative. Words, to start with, are figurative anyway. The people who invented this figurative use, must have had, consciously or unconsciously, in the backs of their heads just one picture, and that was the picture of a wheel which must revolve in order to progress. They did not have the picture of a colt running away, nor the picture of a fire, nor an earthquake, nor a flood—they had the picture of a wheel revolving. For of one thing you may be certain; if these people had not had this picture they would not have used the term in question, they would have used another, since the only time that a word or phrase is used exactly as intended is when it is first invented. Such is the agony of the human mind to make itself articulate and lucid—two things, of course, it can never completely become—that the parturition of a word or phrase is no light affair. We treat these children of the brain lightly only after they have been with us for a long while.

The men who first used the simile, or metaphor, revolution, had in their minds the picture of a wheel revolving and at the same time going forward, and therefore they had, of course, a correct philosophical notion of one of the two great processes whereby mankind steps forward at all—the human process as opposed to the natural one. Revolution, when you come to think of it, is merely the word evolution with an *r* added, and if this be somewhat far-fetched, since, although the root of the words is the same, evolution means to unroll, not simply revolve, revolution, none the less, is one-half of the whole of which evolution is the other part. And the whole is growth. Evolution is nature in growth; revolution is growth with the human mind applied to it. When the farmer in the spring turns up the earth with a plow he is a revolutionist. What is back of evolution we do not know, what is back of revolution is the human will and human thought and imagination. Between them lies all of development; without them nothing happens at all.

Now, nature may unroll—that is, it may as far as we can see, go forward, wastefully and tragically, but none the less forward, without retracing its steps, but man cannot do that. Man is impatient and fallible, and invariably in going forward, sooner or later leaves the main track and discovers himself in a blind alley. He is like a man cruising through an unknown forest, and like this man—that is, if the man is a wise frontiersman—mankind in general, despite all its folly, possesses enough instinctive woodcraft to turn back when it finds itself completely lost. It tries to get back to where it made the wrong turning. That, you can say, is waste time, and so it is, but it is either that or death. Progress, anyhow, is measured along the main road, whatever that may be, and not along the blind alleys.

In short, revolution is constant motion and turns upon itself.

But there is an even clearer and more accurate picture, it seems to me, than that of the wheel. Revolution, or progress, resembles a gigantic weight swinging around an axis that gradually moves upward. You can produce the same phenomenon in miniature by tying a piece of string, with a lead attached, to your finger, and then making the lead rotate, all the while raising your finger almost invisibly. The lead is never still. It is no sooner up than it is down; it no sooner reaches its zenith than it begins to descend once more to its nadir. Apparently it gets nowhere, for it always moves in a circle and the arc of the circle is the same. Progress is not discernible unless you watch the finger, and then only if you watch the finger closely.

The unthinking are those who watch only the arc of the circle; the pessimistic are those who regard only the recurring nadirs, or, if they realize the zeniths at all, see them only as vanishing-points in time; the wise are those who keep their eyes on the finger. In other words, if there is any progress at all, it must be in the shape of a series of bisecting circles, each succeeding one slightly higher than its predecessor. People forget that when they complain of contemporary folly.

If you agree with this figure you will perceive, of course, at no period cause for final despair. You may be living in a nadir, and the nadir of any given era—eras extending over many years, sometimes centuries—is unquestionably lower than the zenith of that era, or of the era that preceded it, or the era that will follow, but at the same time it is higher than the nadir it has succeeded, even if only slightly higher. For instance, it seems to me fairly clear that at present we are living in a nadir, or else approaching it rapidly, which means that simultaneously, of course, immense new forces are at work that will soon be used in the upward pull, and this nadir resembles startlingly, as has often been remarked, the nadir following the Napoleonic Wars. It resembles that nadir in countless ways—in morals, in manners, in costume, in customs, in a frankness, mostly excellent, but frequently abused. Yet at our worst we are a trifle better than were our ancestors of the time of George the IV of England or Charles the X of France, and this world is minutely a better place to live in. Dishonest as we are, we are more honest; vulgar as we are, we are less vulgar; dirty as we may be physically, we are cleaner; and we know more.

I say we are in a nadir, despite our younger critics and philosophers who think they have actually accomplished revolution, for the forces gathering for the upward pull must not be confused with the pull itself. As far as I can make out, we are still in the nadir of the Victorian period, just as, following the Napoleonic Wars, the world was still in the nadir of the eighteenth century. The world did not become instantly modern with the French Revolution, and to-day the extremest modern is still under Victorian influences. His antics are not yet those of the real explorer, but are those of the captive struggling to be free.

This, then, is real revolution, this constant swing upward and downward, this constant movement, and the one thing the real revolutionist cannot do is to stop, is to become static. He never runs things out. If he does, automatically, he ceases any longer to be a revolutionist.

If you are a tiny particle on a rotating globe,

you either go around with the motion of the globe or else you fly off into space, and the latter is what invariably happens to the pseudo-revolutionist the moment he meets with any sort of success, political, literary, or social. He flies off into space, leaves reality, and becomes a doctrinaire, repeating and mulling over what might once have been discoveries, but which have long since become the property of most of mankind.

You can tell the pseudo-revolutionist by this trait, just as you can tell the real revolutionist, or progressive, by the fact that he, to the contrary, is constantly in the stride of his times. I do not mean that if he happens to live in a nadir he leads that nadir in its peculiar vices; I do not mean that he is not vigorously aware of those vices; but I do mean that he attempts to understand the forces that produce those vices, as well as the forces that produce whatever virtues may be coexistent, and that he goes forward as wisely as he can with his generation. If the world is on a downward swing he attempts to use the motion to accelerate what he knows will be eventually an upward swing, and if the world is on an upward swing he attempts to accelerate the motion toward a zenith.

At all events, he is largely an empiricist in a universe where everything should be judged individually; he is never a final pessimist; he can not be completely a destructionist, although in order to build, preliminary destruction is often necessary; he is never a professional reformer or doctrinaire, and never, under any circumstances, is he contemptuous of life or mankind.

There are other traits that mark infallibly the pseudo-revolutionist, one of them being the fact that he thinks of himself as a revolutionist and is irritated with those who, because they have personalities of their own, or because of a wise uncertainty, or because they are preoccupied with other things, will not surrender themselves completely to his will. He has what is called the Messiah complex. You are either with him utterly or else you are against him. No half-way support will do. He is unable to make use of the subtle variations and the shades of character which distinguish mankind. The real idealist, the real progressive, the real revolutionist seldom calls himself by any of these three names.

Four major insanities brand the pseudo-revolutionist, although there are numerous minor ones. Two of these major insanities I have just mentioned. That the pseudo-revolutionist is a doctrinaire; that he thinks of himself as a revolutionist. Once he is in action the other two major insanities show themselves. His mind is utterly destructive, although he does not know it, so his most elaborate programme is completed without any appreciation of history or human nature and is inevitably as falsely constructive as the man himself. Hampered and condemned by his nature, the pseudo-revolutionist is condemned by the mysterious agencies of evolution as well. Unlike the real revolutionist—the progressive—who, when he has overcome evil, usually has something of good to put in its place, the pseudo-revolutionist is forced into upholding a system as vicious and tyrannical as the one he helped, but at the last moment and selfishly, to upset.

Clichés these thoughts? Yes, most obvious truths are clichés.

There is no real revolution about dethroning a czar and then attempting to make czars of one particular class. The rule of a proletariat, so-called, would be as nonsensical as in the past have been proven the rules of aristocracies, so-called. And events in Russia have proved this to be so. If a farmer plows a field and then does not plant it with seeds suitable to that particular soil and climate, he is a poor farmer and a worse revolutionist. The gestures of thickheaded Toryism are no more absurd than are the gestures of pseudo-revolution; they are, also, no more selfish.

But the pseudo-revolutionist cannot help being destructive, for, as has been pointed out again and again, he suffers from a sense of inferiority so fierce that he fears the world as it is and shudders at the thought of attempting to do anything with the materials at hand. A sense of inferiority is, of course, the basis of all fine work; it is certainly the basis of the progressive mind, since no mind can be progressive and be satisfied either with itself or the world as it is. But the real revolutionist knows something of human nature and is not scornful of ordinary tools, and he checks his sense of inferiority long before it becomes the passionate madness of the pseudo-revolutionary or the persecution mania of the murderer. He is never a superior person, for his necessary sense of inferiority has never reached the point where it compensates by a disdain for others. Nor does success change him. He sublimates his success into further useful action, just as in the beginning he sublimated his sense of inferiority into useful action. Lack of appreciation does not embitter him, while, on the other hand, appreciation makes him, in a large way, even more humble.

Indeed, how can any one knowing these things, and to-day every thinking man knows them, continue to use the vague and universal word revolution as it is used at present? How does any one ever dare to use it as a reproach to others or a compliment to himself? Revolution has meant a thousand various attitudes; it has included practically all forward-thinking men. The man who builds a new canal is a revolutionist, the novelist who persuades a generation, the man who invents a new machine.

I do not imply that outside of their specialty these men, through laziness or ignorance, may not be extremely backward, but I do imply that if they are progressive along one line they are revolutionary-minded and could be made progressive along all lines if properly approached. Meanwhile, they should not be called fools, cowards, or numbskulls. Here is a list at random—a brief and partial list—of real revolutionists:

Plato, Aristotle, Praxiteles, Galen, Buddha, Saint Paul, Erasmus, Chaucer, Rabelais, Marco Polo, Columbus, Christopher Marlowe, Shakespeare, Sir Walter Raleigh, Albrecht Dürer, Holbein, Fra Angelico, Saint Francis, Domingo de Guzman, John Knox, Calvin, Ignatius de Loyola, Pizarro, Cromwell, John Bunyan, Cervantes, Copernicus, Voltaire, Frederick the Great, Newton, Washington, Burke, Lincoln, Romain Rolland, Edison, Masefield, Freud, Jung, Einstein. Passionate men, all of these, caught up, one way or another, rightly or wrongly, with a desire for an increase of knowledge, of beauty, and of human dignity even when, to some of them, these seemed to lie in amalgamation with a stern god.

And how greatly each one of them would have disliked the word revolutionist as applied to himself. Washington disliked it; so did Cromwell. They saw themselves merely as restorers of the rights of mankind.

There have been times—but not so often when you reflect upon them—when, in the history of the world, tyranny has been so intrenched that bloodshed alone spelled freedom; but invariably the men who first made the revolution were peaceable men who resisted bloodshed up to the last moment and were astonished and dismayed when they woke up to discover themselves pushed to the last extremity. Unfortunately in the majority of cases these same men have suffered later on for their moderation, just as they suffered for their moderation under the destroyed tyranny. They have had their heads cut off or they have been lined up against a wall and shot. The pseudo-revolutionists, being fools, outnumber the wise and in troublous times are likely to seize power. But not always. They failed in our American revolution, they failed in Cromwell's revolution, and they failed in the recent German revolution. The real revolutionists were in control and much time was saved and much nonsense avoided.

The younger generation seems to forget that Wordsworth and Shelley and Keats and Byron were revolutionists; revolutionists who initiated the romantic freedom of the early Victorian period from whose later tyranny, when freedom had degenerated into convention, the youthful rebels of to-day are escaping. The men who imposed the feudal laws upon the chaos of early Europe were as much revolutionists as were the men who eventually broke feudalism down. The two men, Bernard Shaw and H. G. Wells—like them or leave them, it's true—who have more than any others, save Einstein and Freud, in the past twenty years affected the thought of the English-speaking peoples and through the English-speaking peoples the thought of the world, have steadfastly refused since their extreme youth to call themselves revolutionists. They have been real revolutionists, changing constantly their points of view to meet new conditions. It was Shaw who first made valid the truth that the man who does not change his view-point from time to time is a fool. Before then, consistency at all costs was considered a jewel.

Indeed, so far as I can make out, the only race that has ever thoroughly understood as a whole the meaning of the word revolution has been the Irish, and with the Irish, the meaning of revolution has been understood from the beginning. The most intuitive race there is, the Irish arrived at this knowledge, more, I dare say, by the processes of intuition than by those of ratiocination, but that is unimportant since the conclusion is correct. Revolution to the Irish means "the outs" against "the ins," and although this can be carried to an extreme and is perhaps more useful in other fields of life than the political one, it is based on the well-founded instinctive belief of the ordinary man that those in authority need watching. They do, and Lincoln said the same thing when he announced that he was doubtful if any man was quite good enough to have much power over his fellow human beings. In the Episcopal Church the need for this watchfulness is recognized by prayer. And this brings me to what I have been wanting to say all along, for if the Irish philosophy of revolution, boiled down to its sane fundamentals, is not the democratic theory of checks and balances, of the rights of the minority, of a government sensitive to public opinion, I do not know what is.

Whoever is in authority, revolutionist or reactionary, requires supervision. Only a genius of humility can be trusted with absolute power.

In other words, in the present state of affairs, considering the present sum of human knowledge, the real revolutionist is the real democrat. Beyond that he cannot go; he has not yet sufficient experience or intuition. If he goes beyond that point he ceases to be a real revolutionist and becomes a pseudo one. Within the democratic system lies all the opportunity for change or intelligent revolution man will need for many centuries to come. It is the system that should be perfected, not the theory that should be changed.

The perfect revolutionist is the man—and there were any number of them—who, in the time of the French Revolution, let us say, assisted in the necessary upsetting of the old régime, but just as stubbornly opposed himself to the monstrous tyranny of Robespierre. In short, such a man as Lafayette was to begin with, and when you have described Lafayette as he was to begin with you have come pretty near to describing a democrat. Insolent authority, whether it be the authority of a dictator, of a political clique, of a millionaire, of a beggar, of a trades-union, of a combination in restraint of trade, of an upper class or a lower class, of a church or an atheist, stirs instantly the resentment of the real democrat, and in a democratic country he has the weapons to cure such insolence, even if to seize and use them require time and patience.

What more can be asked of revolution I do not know, and it is certain that at present there is no other plan of revolution that will or can give more.

But there is a vast difference between being

theoretically or fundamentally a democrat, as most Americans are, even if they do not exactly know what the term implies, and being practically a democrat, as so many Americans have ceased to be. And in the difference lies, as I have said, a growing danger not only to this country but to the theory of revolution upon which it was founded. Outside of America, democracy to-day stands on trial. It becomes, therefore, increasingly the duty of America, still believing in democracy, to demonstrate that within the democratic system lies so much of revolution that any other political form is eternally unnecessary—a hope that may be beyond the bounds of probability, but is certainly not beyond those of possibility.

In his next to last book, "The World of William Clissold," H. G. Wells says: "I shall look to America rather than Moscow for the first instalments of the real revolution." And by this he means more or less the sort of revolution I have been talking about: The revolution that can take place within the democratic system. An orderly and peaceful revolution leading toward a general intelligence, a higher form of living, a completer mastery of life. And Wells's revolutionists are the revolutionists I have had in mind—the big-minded business man, the inventor, the scientist, the artist, and the ordinary educated man of a released public. After all, admitting our numerous faults, some of which may lead to disaster unless they are righted, we have already done several things to prove the worth of democracy and to demonstrate its flexibility. We have, for one thing, demonstrated that the average man can lead a life of an amplitude, dignity, and decency undreamed of elsewhere. The native American lacks perspective upon his own country, the inevitable result of too close a view. But ask some American who has been here only a few years what he finds that he was unable to find elsewhere. These people have a secret the native American cannot possess except by inquiry.

Bertrand Russell, in some ways the wisest mind in England, credits us with other virtues. We have, he says, conquered the ancient fears that still rule the thought of the rest of the world: the fear of starvation, for instance, of pestilence, of defeat in war. We are the first race that has achieved the point of view that man is master of his fate and need not submit tamely to the whims of inanimate nature or the follies of his own kind.

And he adds: "To my mind the best work that has been done anywhere in philosophy and psychology during the present century has been done in America."

We begin to get a different survey from that of the professional boob-hunter and pseudo-revolutionist.

But there is another clause that must be tacked

on to all this if a country is to be really great. This release of the ordinary man must be accompanied sooner or later by the release and production of the extraordinary man, not only in business but in every art and every aspiration. Our critics say we are not doing this, and that it can not be done; that the very release of the ordinary man means the suffocation of the man who might, in happier circumstances, be unusual. Outside of the fact that to those who watch it closely and sympathetically, America, with added impetus each succeeding year, seems to be more and more disproving this argument, the argument is based on a false premise physically and historically.

The release of anything, whether it be the release of an explosive or of vast masses of a population, is for a while confusing, discomforting, and disquieting, but in the end what is worthwhile comes even more strongly to the surface. Consider for a moment the question of standardization, and let us try for a moment to be really sensible about it. Standardization is another word that is being used as a bogy to frighten children.

For a number of years most thinking people have been in rebellion, one way or another, against the growing powers of standardization, and with reason, for to protest against a great force, largely uncontrolled, largely blind, and frequently selfish and hypocritical, is the only way to produce eventually some control, some vision, and some honesty.

To protest against such forces, to criticise them, to try to adapt them to better uses and make them more rational is, up to a certain point, the duty of the real revolutionist—that is, the democrat, the individualist—and the real revolutionist, in company with most sensitive people, detests the present or middle stage of standardization, with its ugliness, its stupidities, and its absurdities, but at the same time he should regard standardization with a degree of perspective.

Standardization means no more than the raising of the general level, and it can no more submerge the unusual man or woman than a lake, the waters of which are rising, can submerge a well-built boat. The unusual man and woman go higher and, after the first moments of confusion and possible consternation, are spurred to greater efforts. The people who are submerged are not unusual. To be sure, the unusual man or woman cannot help being frequently irritated; it is necessary to keep an eye on the end. The rows of little houses, all alike, all with the same kind of noiseless plumbing and noisy plate glass, that now injure the American landscape are admittedly less picturesque than the thatched cottages of the English countryside, but they are much more likely some day to produce unusual men and women, most of whose descendants will live in houses just as picturesque as the English cottages, minus rheumatism and filth.

The lively minded grow impatient with the slowness and waste of this process, but their alternatives are not sensible; are invariably anachronistic. Medicine long ago discovered that so long as there were slums and plague spots in the world there could not be a high level of general health and that even the immensely strong were crippled and subject to sudden and unnecessary death. Mr. Mencken's superman is a fascinating plaything, but as childish as the original model of Nietzsche. That is not the way supermen are produced except according to the old specifications, and the old specifications have been tried for centuries and found wanting. The blood, misery, and ignorance of the majority will not produce the supermen of the future.

For the same reasons that I object to the careless use of the word revolution I object to the careless use of the word reaction, although I lack the space to elaborate these reasons. The reactionary is frequently merely a wise man who prefers to go forward slowly, salvaging whatever seems good to him from the past. He, too, is likely to be a passionate man, inherently a revolutionist. And one thing is certain, if he maintains wisely his position, asserting some good in the past, but attempting to understand and assimilate what there is good in the present—sooner or later the world will swing back more or less to where he stands. He may not live to see this reversal, but his grandsons will, and if these grandsons are revolutionists their revolution more than likely will be along the lines for which their grandfather was called a reactionary.

There is nothing, for instance, more amusing than the belief of our present pseudo-revolutionists that they are driving from the world God, mystery, transcendental philosophy, poetry, and gentleness. These things will come back, although, naturally, not quite in the forms in which they were once known.

A new word should be invented to describe that element of humanity with which both the real revolutionary, or progressive, and the real reactionary, or conservationist, are constantly at war. The real revolutionist and the real reactionary are in the motion of life; their enemy is staticism, which is death, whether this staticism take the form of an idiotic and frequently selfish optimism, or a sneering and frequently selfish pessimism. The real revolutionist and the real reactionary are honest and open-minded men engaged as much as possible in the search for truth, and right or wrong as their methods may be, that gives them, if they but knew it, a bond of the deepest sympathy. The man they are out for is the liar, conscious or unconscious, the time server, deliberate or made so by circumstances, the frivolous, made so by vanity or egotism or contempt. Such a man might be called an inertia-ist, for actually his one object, whether he be a pseudo-revolutionist or a pseudo-conservationist, is, once he has obtained a certain position, to maintain at all costs the status quo good or bad. For him the status quo is necessary, for, in the former case, if it alters he is out of a job, and in the other, he wishes to leave you with the status quo while he goes untroubled about his devious and small pursuits.

The deceptive real-estate agent and the deceptive intellectual are very much like those unwilling young mothers who give a stranger a baby to hold and then disappear forever. In the former case, you are given a bundle of cheerfulness, in the latter, a bundle of gloom. In neither case is your mind constructively occupied.

But inertia-ist is a clumsy word, and I am not sure that a few years ago, with what admittedly was a stroke of genius, a word exactly expressing this type of mind, left wing or right wing, was not thrown into the English language. I mean the word Babbitt, and that brings us back once more to that genial family and its ramifications.

I have never seen Babbittry exactly defined, but I think what it means is fairly clear. It is not a matter of class or education. A king can be a Babbitt, and most of them are. I must take issue with Mr. Mencken, although he is supposed to be an authority on the subject. His definition, "A generic name designating the more stupid, sentimental, and credulous sort of business man," seems to me extremely inadequate. It implies the gross error, so many intellectuals fall into, of imagining that it requires no brains to be materially successful. To be successful in anything requires some sort of brains and character, despite the small amount of competition in cleverness. George F. Babbitt is not really a stupid man. He would not be worth bothering about if he was. Babbittry means more than stupidity, it connotes a certain kind of shrewdness, deliberate or otherwise. The real Babbitt is a man who uses valid human emotions and ideas for his own ends without a thought of ultimate truth. It is, for instance, not Babbittry to adore your mother if she happens to be adorable—many intelligent men do—it is only Babbittry when this affection is used for commercial and standardized purposes, as has been the case sometimes in this country. National Smile Week and National Day-dream Week are Babbittry at its worst, but it isn't Babbittry to smile or even, occasionally, to day-dream. Plain sentimentality is always folly, and to be sure it supports Babbittry and nourishes it, but until it is used for ulterior purposes it is not Babbittry itself.

Babbittry, therefore, is deception, whited-sepulcherism in whatever form it is found, whether the whitewash be sentimentality or cleverness. It is a denial of man's supposed preoccupation with the truth; it is more than that—it is a denial that the truth is worth hunting for or that, unknown as it is, it even exists. And this state of mind leaves its visible marks. The man who adopts Babbittry begins to look like a Babbitt, and insensibly his speech, as is the case with all those engaged in evasion, whether consciously or not, becomes a lingo, cant talk, as secretive and special as was the cant talk of the beggars of the Cour des Miracles. On the one hand we have the hearty, meaningless good wishes and the not so unmeaning propaganda of the go-getter, and on the other—well, let me give you a few examples:

"Barnum has almost become a common name. He is a world-synonym for camouflage, bulling, sucker-baiting. In Europe his name connotes America from heel to hair. His soul will go marching on long after John Brown's is pickled in oblivion. And this is because Phineas T. Barnum was born of the very roots of two of our most elemental characteristics—to fake and to clown."

"The gaudy eloquence that bathed the poor Frogs during the late crusade for democracy exaggerated their natural weakness in a truly lamentable manner. . . . One might plausibly argue, indeed, that the complete disappearance of France would produce no more perturbation in the world than the loss of an ear produces in a man."

"To the phenomena of life which surrounds him, the American responds with clock-like precision in one of two ways; to wit, on the one hand, with an Hooray, or, on the other, with a Go to hell."

"When a woman wakes up suddenly in the middle of the night and sees a ghost pointing a ghastly finger at the ceiling, or mayhap only at papa's union suit on the back of a chair, let the ophthalmologist jump into his Buick, rush to the scene, and ascertain, by careful examination, just what has affected the functional delicacy of the optic nerve."

You perceive the similarity of these excerpts to the methods of the backwoods evangelist or the go-getting salesman? The similarity in fundamental spirit and expression? There is the same half-contemptuous use of big words and familiar locutions in the belief that somehow they create wit, the same contempt of the truth, the same lack of any qualifications, the same unfair tactics, the same gesturing and posturing, the same conviction that if you shout long enough you'll be believed. And unfortunately the last is based on a real knowledge of human psychology.

Between the incantations—"How's the big fellow?" followed by the incantatory laugh, or the incantation, "Be sure your sins will find you out," and the incantations, "Wow, Americano, vox mazuma, Homo Americanus," and so on, I see no practical difference.

Let me give you another quotation:

"I'm a pretty conceited guy. I like to think that in every corner of this grand and glorious republic, wherever chewing-gum is sold, there are men, and women, and little children who look for my stuff every month.

" 'Who knows,' say I to myself, 'but what that light gleaming out of yonder farmhouse' "——

But I can't go on.

And what do you think that is? The copy of some advertising Babbitt who thinks if he calls you by your first name he'll be able to sell you something? Not at all. That is the beginning of a book review in a popular magazine which professes to represent the wit and humor of the American uni-

VII

GALLIC CALM

VII

GALLIC CALM

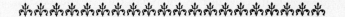

WERE I to select a devil for the purposes of international misunderstanding—that is, if I believed in personal devils, which I do not—I would be hard put to it to chose between the devil of sentimental hatred and the devil of sentimental admiration. Indeed, the latter, although not so likely to end in any obvious evil such as war, for everyday use is a more difficult devil than the former, more sly, more pawkish, much more subterranean. Which brings me to the point that, of all present-day international relationships, the relationship of France and America is probably the most sentimental.

Sentimental in the ordinary way, in the ways of ignorance, prejudice, and scorn, common to the vast majority of the citizens of any country when they think of another; sentimental in an especial and extraordinary way because, apart from these ignorant and prejudiced citizens, there has always been both in France and America a body of thought, minute in the former, large in the latter, given to the very opposite extreme of fulsome and not always sincere compliment. The American friends of France, who sometimes begin the preceding five words altogether with capitals, and from whose war propaganda France and America are still suffering, are quite as capable of doing harm to France as France's enemies; the harm the average French friend of America can do is limited only by his fortunate lack of numbers. To descend from what are obviously serious matters to what seems obviously a trivial one, but which is not trivial, since, in their effect, few things are, the good American women who insist, as thousands of them do, upon the superior charm, civilization, and so on, of French life and Frenchmen are not only discounting the exigencies of a different civilization and environment—the American—which may produce virtues of its own, but, far from accomplishing their object, are as a rule merely turning the American male listener toward a grim irritation.

If your friends are not sufficiently charming and civilized it may be well to tell them so tactfully; otherwise how can they improve? But such advice should always be straightforward and not one of comparison. You should say: "You are not sufficiently civilized; you are not sufficiently charming." You should never say: "Why aren't you as charming and civilized as the French?" If nothing else, the latter is bitterly unfair to the people you are praising.

On the whole, I think my devil would, in this instance, wear the prettiest of Parisian clothes, male or female, interlard his speech with a few French phrases, terribly mispronounced, talk a good deal about manners and sophistication.

This has been true all through history. Franco-American relations, because of this aloofness from reality, have always had a curious habit of oscillation between the exaggerations of sentimental affection and the exaggerations of sentimental hate. Not once have the two nations settled down to look each other squarely and amicably in the face. Their attitudes toward each other have always been filled with self-consciousness and rodomontade of one sort or another. Yet here are two great nations—peculiarly grave and earnest nations—who in a round half-dozen ways, traditionally, by their philosophy of life, very especially by, at least, their surface manners and points of view, should understand each other better than most. Or perhaps, as I have said elsewhere, since understanding, where races are concerned, is perhaps too much to expect, two races who should tolerate each other and like each other better than most.

They have to begin with a theory in common,

yet it is undoubtedly this very tradition of a theory in common, minus any attempt at actual and friendly analysis, that has done much to maintain sentimental and inhuman relationships between France and America. France assisted at the birth of America not only with armies but, long before that, through the philosophies of her men of letters; America assisted the birth of modern France by her own revolution, although the French Revolution proved too bloody and drastic for the less logical American mind, just as French democracy, in its essence, proved too democratic.

Again and again America has blossomed with tri-colored cockades, and France has been draped with American flags, and although the emotions aroused at such times have been real, just as the tradition of a theory in common is real, they have been far too temporary and mere chaff in the face of succeeding gusts of ill-temper. The work of a Jefferson, a Franklin, a Lafayette, a Rochambeau, is only partly done if war, however short, follows within three decades; if a Citizen Genêt can turn liking into loathing. The work of a Lindbergh is little more than a beautiful interlude if within three weeks the French newspapers can resume their complete misunderstanding of our attitude toward the war debts. Perhaps this attitude is wrong, perhaps it isn't, but at all events, right or wrong, it has never been understood.

The tradition of a theory in common, tricolored cockades, friendly flags may be excellent things, but they would be considerably more excellent if the latter were merely the decorations of some sort of inner comprehension and if the former was amplified and made fairly secure by a sympathy based not upon a theory but upon mutual investigation. Indeed, as I have indicated, the tradition of a theory in common may be worse than nothing if it leads only to undue expectations and their subsequent unnecessary disappointments. To fall or to be pushed from a high place is as fatal as to be buried in a cellar. Had France, in the early years of the nineteenth century, really caught the drift of American democracy, she would have understood that, however grateful we might be for Yorktown, we could not altogether stomach a Robespierre or a Napoleon; had we really caught the drift of French character in 1918, we would not have been so dismayed in 1919.

In this respect, and much as they need improvement and elucidation, Anglo-American relations are on a more solid basis. The English and ourselves are not much given to flattering illusions concerning each other, while our unflattering illusions break down at the slightest personal touch. Almost every Englishman has a pet American or two, and is willing to have more, and almost every American finds himself in the same position. For more than a century America and England have got along fairly will in a grumbling sort of way, and they are likely to continue to get along, despite conflicting interests and despite the alarming hints of Commander Kenworthy and some of our own naval experts.

Outside of the fact that for every ton of English or American high explosive shot into or dropped upon New York or London a million or so of English or American foreign-invested capital would disappear, England and America recognize too well each other's failings for any final misunderstanding. They have no lofty pedestal from which to descend and comparatively few abysses of blind prejudice from which to creep.

Much as they may, in times of peace and when they are idle, dislike to admit a common humanity, to the average English mind and American mind, the thought of mutual combat calls to the surface the same inherent distaste as the thought of eating monkeys. Wriggle as much as we may, these people are like us.

Do not mistake me. I am not underestimating sentimental hatred or overestimating sentimental admiration. Hatred, carefully cultivated, is always dangerous, as was proven by the prewar attitudes of France and Germany, while sentimental admiration in the case of France and America is, as I have pointed out, confined to comparatively small, although powerful groups, in both countries, and is not likely to end in dramatic disaster because, fortunately, French and American interests do not clash in any important particular. This does not prevent, however, the same sentimental admiration from being the sly, pawkish, subterranean evil I have described it as being, nor keep it from accomplishing the ultimate object of all international misunderstanding, whether it end in dramatic disaster or not, which is the preventing of any sort of mutual good-will based upon reality.

To try to assess any nation, your own or another, is a gigantic task, but where France is concerned the task is peculiarly gigantic for the American because, added to the delusions that the northerner cherishes for the southerner, or vice versa, the American carries about with him the weight of English-speaking tradition, and for a thousand years England and France have been rivals. An emigrant ship carries much more than its passengers, its crew, and its freight: it carries an infinitude of ghosts and a cargo of transplanted imponderables. What the American thinks of France is confused by what the Englishman of two hundred years or so ago thought of France, confused, even, by what the Englishman of to-day thinks of France.

The whole question of international relationships needs, of course, entire revision from the bottom up. And when I say international relationships, I mean the relationships between the average citizens of the various countries. Relationships that we are slowly beginning to realize, since the war, are by far the more important ones. Nowadays governments can make fools of themselves, and no terrific harm may result; it is only when governments make fools of the average citizen that witches ride.

International thought, not only diplomatically and politically but in the common and paramount sense in which I am using it, lags far behind any other kind of thought. If the average citizen of France and America entertained in his religious beliefs, his medical theories, and his business dealings the same ideals he entertains toward, in the first instance, America, or, in the latter, France, he would still be believing in magic, leeching, and the use of barter instead of currency. He would be using forked sticks to find water and, when his cows refused to give milk, would be hunting mischievous fairies. Of the half dozen or so leading thoughts the average American has about France, all but about one are utterly wrong. They are not only wrong but the exact opposite is true. Of the half dozen or so leading thoughts the average

Frenchman has about America, all are wrong. The preponderance in favor of the American is due to no superior intelligence, merely to the fact that the American travels more than the Frenchman and that the Frenchman, being a European, is always wrong where America is concerned. That is part of the penalty of being a European, whatever the advantages may be.

Roughly speaking, French opinion of America falls into three classes: Either we are still the idealistic and austere republicans of Beaumarchais and Lafayette, the living exponents of Rousseauism—simple, virtuous "*paysans du forêt de la* Pennsylvania," as Hendrik Van Loon says in his history of America—or we are the gangling, ingenuous but shrewd Yankee of such comedies as "Pas sur la Bouche," or we are the more up-to-date materialist of the French popular novel and the French comic weeklies; the gold-toothed—shades of the American dentist with his porcelain fillings!—China-blue eyed, expressionless materialist who, although usually drunk in Paris, is given to bloodless experiments in sumptuary law and savage demands for blood-stained money. Needless to say, the first opinion is held by only a few, and those few have never visited America—royalists for the most part, who, although they do not love democracy, so hate their own government that ours seems a Utopia in comparison. There are certain royalists who are not to be argued out of the belief that New York is a city whose morals are as spotless as its streets are clean. Oddly enough, it is almost as embarrassing to be overpraised for virtue as to be overcondemned for vice.

The second opinion is a survival of the 1880's and 90's, although "Pas sur la Bouche" is a very modern musical comedy. It represents the tolerant amusement of a non-travelling bourgeoisie; the tolerant amusement, not unfriendly, of a period when Americans were quaint but by no means important. The third opinion is the present popular and growing one. We complain, and rightly, of the way history is frequently taught in the American school, but now and then one has illuminating glimpses of the way history must be taught in French schools. A young friend of mine, a representative of a very great French family, told me he thought it a pity France and America misunderstood each other so greatly and that perhaps the trouble began because, after France had given us our country—I quote his words—we, in gratitude, had not given Canada to France.

"But," I said, "Canada was never ours to give."

"Oh, you could easily have taken it."

"Have you never heard of General Montgomery and our army that just got away with its shoes?"

"No, but Canada is really altogether French. The people would have been with you."

Here was ignorance so massive that there was no use combating it. My informant had never heard of the French-Canadian attitude during the war; he believed that most of the Canadian regiments had been French—he had seen them; "big, black-haired fellows talking French"—he was not aware of the French-Canadian feeling toward modern France because of the latter's supposed atheism. And he concluded his argument by a statement which in a few words summed up the difference between European political thought, and action, and American thought and procedure.

"Well, you were very clever," he mused. "First you combined with the English and drove us out of America—which, after all, we really discovered, explored, and settled—and then, that accomplished, when you were ready you drove out the English." That there were no Americans in 1759 had not occurred to him, nor that the whole proceeding credited American international thought with a subtlety totally foreign to it. But in Europe it is quite customary, as we all know, to lay plans in 1900 which will bear fruit in 2010.

Ignorant as the average American is of France, the stock Frenchman, at any rate, has disappeared from our comic weeklies, our newspapers, our novels and our stage. He lingers only in our motion-pictures, and altogether rightly a few months ago the French motion-picture producers protested against this caricature. But what of the American as he appears in all the French vehicles of opinion mentioned, especially the French novel, since novels are supposed to be written by men peculiarly well informed? The French novelist ceases to think at all when an American is introduced. He reaches into his memory and pulls out a type as absurd as it is far-fetched.

The sub-hero of a recent very popular French novel, "La Gondole aux Chimères," by Maurice Dekobra, is a young American, obviously a graduate of Harvard and a member of one of Boston's better families, fortune made in celluloid—it is always celluloid or chewing-gum—whose manners are a cross between those of a bear and a bull moose. He actually thinks the Lion of St. Mark's in Venice is a real lion. His baggage, described in detail, consists of two wardrobe trunks containing nothing but evening clothes and books on venereal diseases, the implication being that he will not be around in the daytime at all. We are, however, credited with evening clothes, which is considerably more than the English always do for us.

Before me on my desk is a collection of French short stories—"Quarantième Ètage," by Luc Durtain—which deals with life on the Pacific Coast.

Unlike most of his compatriots, Luc Durtain has lived in America and should know it well, but in his principal story the hero who begins, as do all Americans, with a fear of women—sic!—but who, having been flirted with by an American girl more released than most—also, sic!—ends up with complete abandon on the subject, misbehaves himself mildly with a strange young girl at the movies, is almost mobbed, and is condemned to the penitentiary to serve eight years for his offense. Here and there the survival of the Cromwellian spirit in America, when given scope, does produce some curious legal procedure, but I have never heard of an instance quite like this. The hero of another novel, "L'Américaine," is a young American—China-blue eyed, gold-filled teeth—who, marrying a French girl met during the war, attempts to turn her old estate into a modern American farm. The point being that, as an American, he can, of course, have no love of the soil or any feeling for its poetry. A curious reversal of facts when we consider the typical French hatred of solitude, or what we call "the country." And so on, and so on.

But if the Frenchman exhibits an ignorance of America that is bewildering—not only an ignorance but what seems a determination to remain ignorant—the average American, searching his opinions, is little better off. These opinions, as I have said, are a combination of folk-tales, prejudices, and northern complacency. Even the modern subjective historian is not yet aware that nations do exactly what individuals do—that is, attribute to other nations the vices they themselves most fear. It is a common psychological trick. You credit yourself with the virtues you most like, you credit your enemies with the vices you most dread.

To begin with, the Frenchman is not a Latin; he is a tempered northerner. He might be described as a brown-haired man between the extremes of the blond and brunette. Only in the south, and then only in Provence, is he more Latin than Frankish. His traditions, to be sure, are for the most part Latin, so, too, his jurisprudence and his art, even to some extent his religion, but underneath the Teutonic mind is constantly at work. The French love of order and logic, quoted so frequently by Gallomaniacs as Latin traits, are not Latin at all, unless you go back to Rome. A claim that could be made with equal justice by every other European race save the extreme northern ones. These traits are not Latin, they are exclusively French. I know of no other nation that has them.

Certainly no real Latin race, if one can use such definite terms when describing the mongrel thing we call a nation, has the slightest sense of either order or logic. Bayonets do not make order; a sense of order is something innate in a man. If it only functions through force, then it is not a sense of order. But the French like order because they like comfort, and whenever it is necessary to be disorderly in order to gain their ends, they return to order as soon as possible.

They may behead an old lady for possessing a title, but they put back again as speedily as possible the chair in which she liked to watch the sunset. For the same reason they prefer to think logically. To think logically by no means implies that you are thinking sensibly or humanly. That all depends upon what sort of premise you have taken. But logical thinking is the most comfortable sort of thinking, the most satisfactory, if you keep your mind from wandering; it has all its edges tucked in, its form is perfect. And all this—this love of comfort, of logic, the French thrift, to which we will come later, the French appreciation of the moment, of its transitory pleasure, of the possible tragedy lying beyond, the French hatred of waste, whether it be waste of gesture or material—comes, I am sure, from the fact that for more than ten centuries, France, lying in the middle of Europe, has been the battle-ground of the world.

You would like order, too, if you had had very

little of it; you would hate waste if you had seen too much of it; you would snatch at the moment and appreciate its gusto if your history showed that for every good moment ten bad ones were likely to occur. You would husband your strength and resources if constantly war threatened. By the same token, not even excepting America, France is the most pacific country to-day in existence; the greatest warrior nation and at the same time the most pacific. There is no place where war is more hated, and no place where, because of fears that are entirely just, war is more prepared for. But if the safety of France were guaranteed, there is no question in my mind that the world would at last find a real leader toward pacificism; an intelligent leader, a leader who knows all the ways of war and all the devious paths of European diplomacy. For this task America is too innocent, too aloof, too preoccupied; England still too obsessed by the fixation of the British Empire.

That the Frenchman is the most professional of soldiers and therefore the least given to military swank, and that he knows too much of war to love it, is shown by that extraordinary organization the French Army. About the French Army there is none of the sense of a *tour de force* that marked the armies of Germany, where an amiable, nonmilitary people, except for the Prussians, had suddenly been forced into an uncongenial mould. The Frenchman doesn't have to show that he is a soldier; he knows that he is one. And he is not delighted to be a soldier, nor has he anything but a due sense of rank. How could he have more in an army where the youngest private in a regiment may be the brother of the colonel?

The Frenchman is not a Latin, and not because of that, for the real Latin is not in the least what the average northerner thinks him to be, but because of his climate, his history, his blood, and his geographical position, he has few of the traits the northern mind has endowed him with, and which the northern mind associates with southern peoples. He is not frivolous, he is not uncertain, he is not licentious. Furthermore, he can be charted by the northern mind with fair accuracy. The chart will not be the same as the charts of a German, an Englishman, or an American, but it will be completely readable to all three.

The Frenchman is no more a Latin than the Spaniard, who is a Goth and a Celt, except in the south where he is a Moor. The Frenchman is never frivolous; he is steadfastly certain, although his certainty may not always please our fancy; and to take up the question of immorality in its common sense, and to get rid of it speedily, since it is too vexed a question to consider in detail, the

Frenchman, within the limitations he has set himself, is an exceedingly moral man.

An immoral man is a man who has no moral code, or rather, a man who breaks, without much thought, whatever moral code he may have, since, for a man without morals—that is, one who does not know what morals mean—there is another term—"unmoral." The French have a very definite moral code, and more than most people they live up to it. I merely call your attention to the complete sacredness with them of the young girl, the French horror of assault and the almost total absence of the crime on French soil; the French insistence that whatever a man may do he must do it gently and considerately.

Perhaps, as has been said again and again, the Frenchman best shows his stern morality in his conception of the family. Upon this conception the entire French moral code is based. Being a realist, the Frenchman has long ago come to the conclusion that although you cannot be sure of loving the same woman all your life, you can be sure, if you have children, that most of your life you will be a father. To him divorce means the selfish and evil breaking of a compact, and the destruction of an institution. And I am not sure he isn't right.

It is all a question, once more, of whether aspiration, with its inevitable failure, or a fairly perfect accomplishment within strict boundaries is better for you and the world, or not. The former does occasionally bring true gigantic dreams through which humanity steps a prodigious stride forward, but in the meantime humanity is very uncomfortable, exceedingly confused, and much given to beautiful platitudes that have little relation to ordinary procedure. French immorality is more decent—if you can use such a term—than English and American immorality, just as ordinary French life is more decent than ordinary English and American life, but by that very fact it is more hopeless.

The French cannot reconcile English and American opinions and protestations with the New York and London stage, with divorces, newspaper headings, tabloids, cabarets and, in America a recent phenomenon, the score or more of cheap magazines whose interest in sociology of a certain kind is considerably less pleasant than that of *La Vie Parisienne*, or *Le Rire*, and whose performance is infinitely less witty and artistic. But that is because the French, as I have already partially pointed out, cannot by their nature understand the feat, so dear to the ice-breathing peoples, of the reach exceeding the grasp. To the Frenchman, to reach for anything not readily accessible seems silly. This is bound up with his love of comfort, of logic, of sparseness, of good form, and it produces, on the one hand, the orderly charm of French life, and, on the other, the chief failure of the French mind.

The Frenchman is a bad poet; his mind is confined. He is a bad financier because the dollar of the day always looks bigger than the fortune of the future. Until recently he has been a poor empire builder and emigrant, because going to the horizon is uncomfortable, and what is beyond is unknown. France gave away half the North American continent while England, and later America, blindly, vaguely, by no means knowing what they were doing, took it over. France stopped building the Panama Canal because of mosquitoes. But France, until the war, had, within France, the best roads in the world, the neatest countryside—save for England—the best hotels and the best cooking. Nowadays she has none of these things, but that is another question. Choose, however, in your own mind, what does the world more good—empires and canals, or roads, cooking, and hotels. As for myself, I don't know.

The British and American mind works by what can be described only as a series of hunches. The British like to speak of their foreign policy, but in reality that is not a policy at all but a fabric of opportunism. The Englishman and American leap in the dark and then explain afterward—usually on excellent and high grounds—but the Frenchman has a neat theory to begin with and a neat theory with which to end. That frequently these theories have nothing in common is a characteristic of both logic and the Gallic disposition. And so we come to that trait of the French which mystifies us as much as our imagined hypocrisy mystifies them. I mean the close-knit French argument which seems to us often no more than passionate nonsense and unfairness.

Logic, as I have said, may have nothing to do with common sense. It is merely dove-tailing together certain similar thoughts. The Frenchman builds a beautiful cellar and then, in many cases, starts his house twenty feet above the ground. Both cellar and house are excellent, but they may have no connection. Recently I read a masterly introduction, written by one of France's greatest scholars, to a volume of Breton folk-tales. The thesis was that Breton folk-tales are absolutely indigenous, unlike, that is, folk-tales anywhere else, and are marked by a melancholy, gentle, but never horrible. The argument was brilliant, cogent, and conclusive, and I was convinced and interested until I read the folk-tales themselves. Then I discovered that the argument just wasn't true. There was nothing more to be said. It wasn't true. The

French doctor is an excellent man if you are ill according to his theory, but if you have something else the matter with you, you are likely to be unfortunate.

I know a lady who, going to Vichy for no serious cause except to accompany a friend, was examined by a French doctor while covered with bed-clothes.

"When did you begin to take on weight?" he asked.

The lady, alarmed as women always are at such a question, and having gained two pounds recently, murmured: "A month ago."

"Ah, you are very much overweight. I will write you out a regimen. Come to see me in two weeks."

Calling at the office at the appointed time, the lady found a doctor who gasped at her habitual slimness.

"But good Lord," he said, "I might have killed you."

The French present impregnable arguments against paying the American debt, but they leave out entirely the question of whether they borrowed the money, whether America herself was at any time uncomfortable, and whether America herself spent any money. I do not say that these latter points cannot be successfully disposed of; I merely say the French leave them out.

To my way of thinking, then, the Frenchman is not a Latin; he is by no means volatile, he is extremely certain, in so far as he wants to be, and he is the least excitable person I know. Neither his revolutions nor his panics are the result of excitement. They are a combination of lucid thought, a precise knowledge of the value of histrionics, and, not unfrequently, of a skin-saving selfishness. The French Revolution was the most carefully dramatized revolution, rising to an apex of slaughter, the world has ever seen. As for French excitement, observe it—how it arises, how it reaches a climax, how it dies away into instant smiles and good nature, once a point is gained.

Indeed, far from being the impulsive, gesticulatory creature he is supposed to be, the Frenchman, in my opinion, is the most masculine man alive. I realize the horror of the Englishman and American at this statement, but they need not become too indignant. I am not at all sure that complete masculinity is a good thing. I am only sure that the lyric, self-conscious, bemused Englishman, and the confused, easily humbled, aspiring American are far less masculine, according to the common definition of the term, than the assured, hard-bitten, spare Frenchman. Of course, in all such discussions the question of class enters. I am referring particularly to the French peasant and the French upper classes, and where the latter are concerned, to those who live mostly in the country. If any one can show me a harder or better-conditioned man than the French rural aristocrat, I should like to see him. These are hawk-like fellows. But this, after all, is no proof of what I am saying, for the English and American upper classes are well-conditioned, too, and, furthermore, share a love of the country which is anything but a universal Gallic trait. The French show their masculinity by their attitude toward women and their coolness in crises—not bravery, although that is taken for granted, but coolness. Yes, even remembering La Bourgogne and discounting it for the reasons already given, although, in any case the panic of wharf rats means little one way or another.

In no country are women more powerful than in France—I refer you to the position of the French wife in her husband's business affairs—but in no country are they made more to feel that they are women. A very different thing from the aloof power granted them in America. The more masculine a man is the less he fears the interference of women in his life, but the more he insists that they shall always be women. As to French coolness, I can best summarize it by this preference: In a crisis I would rather be with a Frenchman than any man I know, but only if the Frenchman's own safety were involved—not an unimportant qualification. Here is a story slightly beside the point, but fairly illustrative:

During the war a friend of mine was travelling from the Front to a base-camp with a young aviator. In the railway compartment were three French officers and two English majors. For the first half day the French, as usual, were charming, the English, as usual, barely polite. About noon the train stopped on a curve and my friend and the young aviator got out on the wrong side. While they were standing on the track another train rounded the curve, and their own train started. They jumped for the door of their compartment, and as they did so the approaching train hit the door. The young aviator was killed and my friend received a dent in his skull that kept him in a hospital for two months.

At once the attitudes of the French and the English changed. The French, seeing that they could be of no real help, since nurses and doctors immediately appeared, walked away. They did not know these young Americans; in three years of war they had seen enough blood. To the contrary, the two fusty old English majors forgot all about themselves and were, as my friend described them, "tender as women." They never left his side until they saw him safe in a hospital. Practically these services amounted to nothing; spiritually they amounted to a great deal. But none the less, had the Frenchmen been victims of the accident themselves, I would have preferred them as companions. It is my belief that they would have been cooler than Englishmen. I don't mean outwardly; I mean inwardly. The Englishman has trained himself to a wonderful façade. He seldom shows embarrassment or fear, but underneath there is frequently a whirling vacuum. He dies beautifully, but not always sensibly.

The Frenchman is not uncertain, he merely does not wish as much as the Englishman and American. What he does wish, he wishes accurately and to the edge of its carefully charted limits. When he falls short in English and American eyes it is because he has never had any intention of going further. We are inclined to think of him as a bad friend. He is not a bad friend, but because of the tragic and uncertain quality of French history, when friends part they have learned to think of each other only with gentle resignation. Nor is the Frenchman frivolous. He is gay when the occasion demands, but that is a totally different mood. Real gaiety is the antithesis of frivolity. Only people who are aware of the underlying sadness of life are ever really gay. The others are merely noisy. Gaiety, an exquisite thing, always has to it an edge of desperation.

You cannot understand the French at all unless you perceive the fundamental quiet melancholy that pervades them, a melancholy which, once more, is the result of a gray, rather sad climate, centuries of war, the adjustments that have been necessary on the part of a people northern by blood, Latin by tradition, central by location. *Triste* is the only word that will describe the quality I mean. But it is more than that, because it is hardy, and strong, and full of laughter, with a love of life and a vast amusement with it. French music shows this, French poetry, even the French concert hall. When I think of France I do not think of Provence with its blue skies and fierce coloring, for Provence is really Roman, and Grecian, and Moorish; I think of some fountain, beautifully carved, excellently well-ordered, at the end of a long, closely-clipped walk of yew, under a gray day with a trace of rain it it.

Of all the common charges made against the French, there is only one which impresses me as holding water. The Frenchman in money matters is indeed trying. Not dishonest, or at least, not more so than any other nation—that part of the allegation is absurd—but short-sighted, penurious, and suspicious. And just as the manners of the English produce an international distaste for them quite out of proportion to the failing, so does this financial smallness of the French not only injure French perspective but build up about the French folk-tales difficult to combat. Boni de Castellane, in a moment of lucidity, has written: "*Mes compatriotes sont, en general, des gens ordonnés, mais avares et petits, sans reconnaissance pour ce que l'on a fait pour eux,*" or, in other words: "My countrymen are, in general, a well-ordered race, but avaricious and small, without recognition of what one has done for them." On this subject our recent expeditionary force is well supplied with stories. Who has not heard of the keepers of *estaminets* who made a fortune out of our troops and then handed in bills for wear and tear? What billeting or commanding officer is without extraordinary memories?

Yet all this should not be stressed too much. Stupid peasants and small shop-keepers throughout history have regarded alien visitors, especially a visiting army, as lambs ready for the sacrifice. Gratitude, like most virtues, is largely a matter of intelligence. Most of us who have read history remember the letters Rochambeau's army sent home. Extortion, avarice, and a lack of recognition of favors are by no means exclusively French traits.

What the stupid majority of a nation does amounts to comparatively little anyhow; it is what the more released classes do that is impressive, and unfortunately the characteristics just mentioned do not, with the French, diminish as much in proportion to education as they should. That the French are nowadays aware of these vices is, however, a hopeful sign; just as nowadays the French, due partly to a growing vision, partly to an increasing colonial empire, are also aware of their second greatest failing—the failing embraced within the words self-complacency, ignorance of other nationalities, unwillingness to travel, and unwillingness to investigate. The French are beginning to travel; they are beginning to expand. Meanwhile no incident is more interesting racially or more a trifle sad, than a Frenchman extorting a small sum of money from an American. Here are two nations as far apart as the poles in their conception of monetary values. The American is seldom the easy mark he is supposed by the European to be—the curious contradiction who, personally, is so spendthrift, but nationally such a Jew of Venice. About money the American has a mystic feeling unknown to other peoples and, to them, utterly not to be explained—particularly not to be explained to the French. The American has toward petty avarice a Lincoln-like resignation. He knows so well that this mysterious thing to which he alone of races seems to have any sort of philosophical clew will in the end turn upon and destroy the man who treats it not as a symbol but merely as so many coins.

We must not leave these leading characteristics of the French mind on the liability side—characteristics altering, however, as I have said, under the pressure of modern communication—without again calling attention to the fact that they are partly due to France's peculiar and perilous history, and without adding that they also derive to some extent from the reverse side of a virtue. That, of course, is true of most vices as well as most merits. A failing is frequently no more than a virtue over-ridden; a virtue is frequently no more than a conquered vice.

Although the French are not Latins, they have, markedly, one Latin idiosyncrasy. The northerner is a vain man, the Latin a conceited man. Between vanity and conceit lies, as we all know, a world of difference. The vain man is self-conscious, restless and insecure. When he boasts, it is to overcome his uncertainty. The conceited man has no need of self-consciousness; he has his own opinion of himself, and that is all that matters. As a result, for all ordinary purposes the conceited man, provided he is not too conceited, is a much pleasanter companion than the vain man. Nietzsche has pointed out this difference. From this placid self-sufficiency has arisen one of the most beautiful of French traits—that is, when the trait does not result in unfairness to other nations or an unwillingness to learn. The trait I am referring to is French patriotism, that odd, mystic conception of *La Patrie*, which is not the Englishman's passionate love for a small piece of England, nor the American's passionate pride in American achievement. This French patriotism is the purest flame of patriotism which exists and, since it is largely philosophical, it can be as readily turned—although this sounds paradoxical—toward a benign internationalism as now, so often, it is turned toward a fierce provincialism. Once again, the placidly self-assured man, if approached properly, can be a much fairer man than the vain man. He is not so busy making an impression, believing that the impression—a good one—is already made. The Frenchman above all things loves a *beau geste*, because a *beau geste* is frequently a compliment toward some one whom, in one way or another, you admire and wish to please. The *beau geste* of a Lindbergh means more to him than a hundred pages of argument. And he is, of course, right. Stupid people, malignant people, people who wish you altogether harm are incapable of *beaux gestes*. No thoroughly bad man can have really good manners; no thoroughly good man can be wholly without good manners. We have too long confused ourselves with the mediæval conception of manner in contradistinction to manners. Manner is something imposed upon a man. A very evil man may have it. Manners are a combination of intelligence and sensitiveness. It is folly to say a man has good manners but doesn't mean them. He cannot help but mean them. They are a symbol, if nothing else, of his desire to put other people at their ease. That is a good desire.

In this respect the French and the Americans are utterly in sympathy. Both nations are eager to make every one who comes into their presence comfortable. They never mistake rudeness for frankness. They do not think honesty consists of showing distaste. Nor is this merely a surface sympathy. Both French and American manners come also from a complete lack of swank—a word I have used once before in reference to the French Army. Lack of swank is perhaps the finest of French traits. This is not a superficial quality. It lies deep in a man's mind. It is a man's admission that, however highly placed he himself may be, he is no more after all than a man. It is his universal *beau geste* to humanity.

VIII

"NO GENTLEMEN PRESENT"

VIII

"NO GENTLEMEN PRESENT"

SO-and-So, well known in the more revolutionary literary circles of New York, was giving an evening party. This is a true story, not a fable. So-and-So, although very revolutionary, is extremely successful and lives in one of those uptown New York apartments where there is an unsullied Renaissance fireplace in the hall and a carved French prie-dieu covering the telephone. One of So-and-So's guests asked him a question.

"Is What D'you Call Him here to-night?" she said, mentioning the name of a certain author.

So-and-So is a witty man. He looked about him carefully and shook his head. "No," he answered: "No. There are no gentlemen present."

Everybody thought that very funny; as for myself, I thought it tragic. History is often summed up in a sentence; the best of criticism is frequently a phrase. In his brief statement So-and-So described a cult, a social, and literary phenomenon, a danger, what is now becoming a nuisance, however much of a necessity at one time it may have been, and, unwittingly, himself and his friends. Here was a complete summation, but, and So and So did not know it, here also was an accurate boomerang.

That was a year ago. Nowadays I would not find the announcement so tragic. There is every indication that the cult is passing, the phenomenon growing stale, the nuisance abating, and the danger, although in some quarters increasing, in others becoming less. The way things are going, before long So and So's drawing-rooms, for he is nothing if not up-to-date, may be crowded with gentlemen, breathing down each other's necks.

Parrot-wise, shaking our wings, in the manner of the unfortunate bird who inquired, after a bucket of water had been thrown over him, where every one was "when the blamed hurricane struck," we are emerging from a period of hokum-hunting and average citizen-baiting, exactly as twenty years ago we emerged from a period of muck-raking. We are a trifle battered, somewhat leaner spiritually, considerably harder mentally, by no means as foolishly optimistic and self-satisfied as we were eight, or even five years ago. For this increase in grace, small in some respects, larger in others, we have undoubtedly in many ways to thank the hokum-hunters, and to them credit will be given later. Meanwhile, those who cannot recognize this emergence, this increase in sardonic awareness, do not know their own country.

Not that hokum has disappeared. By no means, although it is altering its face and has been forced to become subtler. Not that evil or absurdity are by any possible stretch of the imagination under control. Certainly not. Not that we, like every other nation, are not subject to dismaying passions and to frequent and universal sentimentalities and insanities. But the flatulent hokum which, since the war, has here and there afflicted us, is now so generally recognized by every one who can read or write that even the hokumists themselves are aware of it. For mistaken political or financial or religious reasons they may still cling to their ancient idols, but within their hearts they are uneasy.

Paradoxically enough it would seem, but not in the least paradoxical when you come to think of it, we are not only emerging from a period of average citizen-baiting but we are also emerging from a period of gentlemen-disdaining. George F. Babbitt and the man of gentle breeding and tradition, or his brother, the man of gentle instincts and desires, have all had a hard time of it. Like the parrot, they have been doused with water. Had George Washington been alive to-day, he and George Babbitt would have found themselves bracketed more than once. Indeed, George Washington, dead, has recently been subjected to much the same sort of attack and, were he living, would find himself in even a more baffling and irritating position than George Babbitt.

He would be told he didn't exist, gentlemen being merely figments of the inflamed romantic imagination. A man of flesh and blood, he would be told that spiritually he was a ghost; that all he believed in, tried to live by, used as a standard to pull himself back to after the failures inherent in human nature, were so many hypocrisies, unrealities and wraith-like delusions. In short, that he was a large, peripatetic whited-sepulchre. To the contrary, George Babbitt, who between ourselves never has trod this earth except as a figure of satire, and never will, would be just as heartily assured of his actuality. He would be more than assured, he would be told that he was the perfect image of at least ninety-nine per cent of his fellow citizens.

It is easier, on the whole, to be alive and hated, than to be alive and yet be told you are not there. The wart-hog, for all his ugliness, is better off, could he understand, than the giraffe to whom the astonished countryman denied any place in life whatsoever.

This, then, is the paradox. Not that average

citizen-baiting and gentlemen-disdaining go together, for they always have gone together when hokum-hunting was afoot; not that the same man who castigates George F. Babbitt should also deny the existence of George Washington, or his spiritual descendants, thus placing George F. Babbitt in the dilemma of having nowhere to go should he attempt to better himself; but that the man who castigates George Babbitt and denies George Washington should be unaware of the somewhat obvious fact that he, calling himself a bitter realist, is proclaiming an unreality and at the same time repudiating what is real.

The traits of George Babbitt exist. In some men there are more of them than in others. These traits have deserved the punishment they have received. It is a fine thing that the country is now becoming aware of these traits. But never has there been a man like George F. Babbitt in all this broad and long land. Our next task, now that we have been made aware of Babbittry, is to make ourselves aware that although Babbittry is authentic, a Babbitt is not. It is dangerous to imagine too long that a lay-figure is a man. Men are born, die, do a thousand things where for a few minutes, anyhow, they must be flesh and blood.

Now, nothing takes place without a good reason for it, and if you will reflect for a moment you will readily see why, in the past decade, hokum-hunting has been necessary, why it evolved naturally, and why, as I have said, the hokum-hunter invariably goes after the average citizen and the man of gentle instincts at the same time. And here I must interpolate the fact that when I use the terms average citizen and gentleman I am not using them as antonyms. It is stale news that the average citizen is frequently a gentleman and the so-called gentleman, frequently, not an average citizen, but a sub-average citizen. I am describing a state of mind, not a social condition, and I use the terms merely because they are convenient and represent ideas which, however vague, are in a broad way generally understood.

What is an average citizen? What is a gentleman? Don't be absurd. I know and you know, although neither of us can put our knowledge into words. To ask questions like this is a favorite diversion of a certain type of mind to which, I trust, yours does not belong. If it does, pretty soon you will be asking me to define charm, or beauty, or goodness. Many of the most actual things in the world escape definition. By means of such questions the less scrupulous hokum-hunters throughout history have put out of countenance numerous simple but honest dissenters.

When hokum-hunting is afoot, and in one guise

or another it is usually afoot two or three times in every century, the average citizen and the man of gentle instincts invariably find themselves on the firing-line because hokum-hunting in its essence is an attempt to get back to reality . . . either to get back to reality, or to push forward to reality. This being so, the hokum-hunter finds, of course, among the first and more obvious things to attack those conventions which, however necessary at one time and expressive of a valid sentiment, have degenerated into mere formulæ and sentimentality. It is easy to understand, therefore, without further comment, why the average citizen, and the man of gentle traditions, are the two singled out for the principal hue and cry. Both are more given than others to accepting conventions without question and both find it more necessary than others to live by conventions. The former is true because, more than most, both are steadily busy—yes, even the idlest of idle rich men. The feverish preoccupations of idle rich men are extraordinary. The latter is true because, more than most, the average citizen and the man of gentle traditions have stable positions in the world and, in order to maintain them, must exercise care. They are, in consequence, likely to be more conventional than most men, and they are the most likely to fall into errors due to preoccupation with other things, and so are the first to be attacked, although they are also frequently the first to discover their errors and scramble back to some approximation of the truth.

The American business man has learned considerably more in the past ten years than the Russian communist, and the more honest and intelligent hokum-hunters, realizing that he is learning, are leaving him alone in order to study the hokum of "the proletariat."

Little fault can be found with the honest essence of hokum-hunting. To attempt to rid the world of conventions which, however necessary at one time and expressive of a valid sentiment, have degenerated into mere formulæ and sentimentality, is a worthy undertaking. Without it the world would never go forward, nor would the average citizen or the man of gentle tradition change half as readily as they do to meet changing conditions. It is in the mistaking of the misapplication of an idea for the idea itself that the rank and file of hokum-hunters go wrong. Use is confused with abuse. The qualifying phrase, "however necessary at one time and expressive of a valid sentiment," is overlooked.

The rank and file of hokum-hunters do not say, these conventions to which so many people subscribe have become sentimental, they say, the entire presumption back of these conventions is sentimental. They do not say the average citizen has accepted without reasonable thought sentimental attitudes, they say, the average citizen should be abolished. They do not say, many of the rules that are supposed to govern the conduct of a gentleman are obsolete, they say, the whole conception of what a gentleman is is nonsense. In this they do not hold with the great hokum-hunters.

Cervantes was a hokum-hunter when he wrote "Don Quixote." Chivalry had fallen into decay, was absurd, was a positive evil. But Cervantes never attacked the chivalric impulse which is an immensely fundamental one. Nor did he deny that it was chivalry which had rescued Europe from the Dark Ages. Voltaire, Mirabeau, were hokum-hunters, but neither assumed that at one time a strong central government had not been needed to bring France out of anarchy, nor did they assume that the ideal of a strong central government was nonsense. The native crop of hokum-hunters waste their strength and scatter their efforts. The average citizen and the gentleman are fairly perpetual figures. You can run them into holes, but before long they reappear. Three generations from shirt-sleeves to shirt-sleeves is not half so true as three generations from shirt-sleeves to gentle breeding.

Not only does nothing take place without a good reason for it, but as a general rule no reform occurs except where a virtue has been twisted out of its original meaning. More than this, every virtue twisted out of its original meaning has been, to begin with, no more than an answer to another virtue which, in its turn, was twisted out of its original meaning. This sounds a trifle complicated, but it is not complicated when it is illustrated.

For example, muck-raking was an attack upon over-combination and ruthlessness in business. But over-combination, with its resulting ruthlessness, was originally no more than the wise realization on the part of American business that small competition and small production were wasteful processes. To combine was a step forward, a virtue, it only became a vice, and then not in its essence, when combinations lost sight of their original purpose and grew tyrannical. The muck-rakers won. They, and their like, always do. It is a mistake to imagine that a man can be a business man and a fool. There is no man more ready to learn than the business man. Into American business, and this was accelerated by the war, there now came entirely new ideas. Indeed, most of these ideas had never before entered any man's head. Instead of crushing your competitor, if he were at all intelligent you took him into partnership; instead of insisting upon a great central combination, you used these intelligent partners to establish numerous smaller, fairly self-governing combinations. Instead of the old theory that the smaller the wages the higher the net profits, you began dimly to perceive that the higher the wages and the shorter the working hours, the larger your consuming market. So the American manufacturer began to sell to his own workingmen and, furthermore, to educate his workingmen to like better things. Important as these changes were, however, they were not half so important as the revolution which occurred in the relationship of the seller and the buyer.

Up until the first decade of this century the attitude of the seller, whether he was selling merchandise, public service, or personal service, was the political slogan, "the public be damned," translated into other walks of life. If you met with real service, it was merely a chance happening due to some one individual's progressive intelligence. Any one who fails to recognize the vast amelioration in this respect that has taken place in American life from hotels to railway trains, and from railway trains to the buying of steel rails, is a singularly unobservant person.

But once again a new virtue began to be misapplied, and once more what in the beginning were conventions due to necessary and valid sentiments degenerated into mere formulæ and sentimentality.

There was more to it than this. Almost always a new virtue is subject for a while to the devious intentions of the uncertain or the dishonest who see in it an added opportunity for deception and quick money, and a convenient cloak for their real purposes. When gold is first discovered the mining is a careless process, heaps of débris accumulate, and a number of undesirable citizens congregate. It is only when these heaps of débris are worked over, the undesirable citizens run out, and a stamp-mill set up, that the mining becomes to any degree a real business. If you add to the slogan "service," which was now in the mouths of the uncertain and dishonest, or the criminally careless, the powerful weapons of propaganda and organization for selling purposes, the use of which the war had taught us, you can readily see what opportunities were open to the insincere and self-seeking. How frequently the stupid or ignorant would confuse the letter with the spirit.

The hokum-hunters responded to the need there was for them, just as twenty years before, the muck-rakers had responded to the need there was for muck-raking. And although their path was at first a difficult one, before long it became popular and successful. People generally were tired of gestures that meant nothing and professions of faith unfortified by actual performance. The period of the glittering façade and the inadequate interior began to disappear as two generations earlier the period of the false two-story front had disappeared. Generally people were annoyed by hotels that told you, by means of little cards under the glass of the bureau-top, how much they loved you and appreciated your patronage, and then did nothing to recapture it; generally people were bored by stout gentlemen who arose at club meetings and, with tears in their voices, spoke of charity and good-will when in their private affairs they were, as you knew, totally unscrupulous; generally people had enough of patriots who waved the flag for the sole purpose of selling their goods. Within five years the hokum-hunters found themselves—although most of them did not know it, and do not know it now—persuading a country already persuaded. I doubt if the annual meetings of the journals of protest, or whatever it is they hold, are at present much more sardonic than the weekly meetings of the average Kiwanis Club.

Meanwhile, the fundamental ideas back of the words co-operation and service became no more defunct, are just as valid to-day, as the fundamental ideas back of the words business combination, average citizen, and gentleman. Perhaps other terms for co-operation and service will have to be found since these words have fallen into such contempt, have been so abused and over-used, but the purposes and actualities they express are stronger than they have ever been. They have been cleansed already of a great deal of nonsense. In the future they will be cleansed still more.

It is not, as I have already implied, any longer the average citizen or the gentleman the country need fear. The average citizen is nowadays, and at least for the time being, a fairly forthright and caustic fellow; the average gentleman, save for some extremely ancient or perverted ones, is as little reactionary as he has ever been in his history. Both these men are still selfish, of course. Selfishness is difficult to eradicate. But however selfish they may be, they are at least aware of another side, and are not too solemn about themselves. It is not these two classes that need much further castigation—not at present, although they require, of course, like every other class in the community, constant watching; it is the hokum-hunters who now need opposition, criticism and, where they are worth saving, conversion. They need these things for their own salvation and, much more, for the sake of their country.

They need these things for their own salvation, because upon whether they recognize the change that has come over the country or not, upon whether they recognize or not that satire can only be prolonged so far, depends whether or not they turn, here or there, into artists, or, on the other hand, find themselves relegated to the American wing of the Metropolitan Museum. At this very moment they are in imminent danger of becoming historical curiosities. The word artist, to be sure, has also been as much of a stench in their nostrils as the words gentleman and average citizen. But they will have to get over that, too, since the word artist is just as integral a word as the words gentleman and average citizen. You can't escape from these three words or the attitudes of mind they imply. No matter how often and how deep you bury them, they come again to the surface. While as for the word artist, the attitude of mind it implies is in direct opposition to hokum-hunting. The attitude is invariably one of pity and irony, never one of irony alone. An artist cannot see a man as a symbol, he sees him always as a man. To the artist there has never been and never will be a George F. Babbitt. Frequently artists, being by nature rebels, become, when the occasion demands, hokum-hunters, but they never remain hokum-hunters once the occasion passes. That is a touchstone for the discovery of an artist. Furthermore, the artist heaves a sigh of relief when he can turn from hokum-hunting to his own real business.

One of the most interesting of recent phenomena along this line has been the discovery on the part of Sherwood Anderson of an America he did not know existed—a quaint, kindly, intelligent, individualized America despite all its inevitable provincialisms and prejudices. You can't, however, have everything. Prejudice and some degree of provincialism usually accompany quaintness and individuality, save in the cases of exceptional persons. But Sherwood Anderson, even at his blackest, has always been an artist, so this discovery on his part might have been expected.

Yet it is not, as I have said, by any means the conversion of the hokum-hunters for their own sakes that is of permanent importance, although, for the sake of American writing, it is vitally important; nor are opposition, criticism, or conversion so important domestically. The country, where hokum is concerned, is getting along fairly well. It realizes now that all the ballyhoo, far from being depressing, is, in reality, encouraging; that is, the general public is on the point of understanding that hokum-hunting is, as a rule, not a symptom of essential sin but of virtue misapplied. That it cannot, as a rule, occur except where virtue is. On the whole, the average citizen, the gentleman, every one else, have taken to heart what has been said to them, and have now reached that state of discernment where they are even beginning to disengage reality from satire; where they are even beginning to realize that the hokum-hunters have overstated their case.

No intelligent American, save perhaps the inveterate hokum-hunter, any longer believes that American business is utterly corrupt, American government utterly selfish, American life utterly drab, the American, because of standardization and machinery, or any deliberate or demoniac intention, in danger of losing his soul. They see once more that evil is usually stupidity, therefore altogether human. They see many errors and dangers in all walks of American life, but they do not believe in any perfect or overwhelming evil. Above all, they do not believe that America has not just as many gentle, idealistic, and well-bred people as any other country, or that the artistic impulse in America is either dead or materialistic. They no longer believe these things, and they are right. But, on the other hand, Europe, casting about for reasons to condemn us that will look more sympathetic and logical in print than a quarrel over debts and an uneasy dislike of a younger nation's sudden rise to power, has found these reasons ready-made. If you will go back a little into history you will discover that almost every national vice now attributed to us by European observers was first made public and exaggerated by an American hokum-hunter. Almost every vice, that is, save the fact that we are a democracy which, to a certain type of European mind, is in itself—ipso facto—the vice from which all others flow.

This outer aspect of hokum-hunting, this exportation feature of it, as it were, is a very important matter. A very vital matter. In many ways the future hangs upon it. It is what I especially want to talk about.

No wonder Europeans think Americans utterly materialistic, enough Americans have told them so. No wonder Europeans think there are few gentle, or well-bred, or idealistic Americans, and that these few make not the slightest impression on American life. Have not enough Americans assured them of this? No wonder they think we are becoming a nation of mechanical monsters.

Now you know, and I know, what all this is about. We are able to discriminate and to disentangle the true from the false. We know that we have largely earned this domestic condemnation and we are thankful it has occurred, but we also know that for a nation to be able to criticise itself in such a universal fashion as America has done in the past decade is in itself a final proof that the nation cannot by any possible chance be a millionth part as evil as it calls itself. Self-criticism is a sign of awakening self-consciousness. When evils are so powerful and intrenched as to be actually prevalent and expressive of the innate genius of a people, there is no criticism save here and there a single persecuted voice. Under such conditions hokum-hunters do not grow rich, fat, and famous as they have done in America. But if we know all this, the foreigner doesn't, or, at least, in the present perilous condition of the world, he doesn't want to. Unconsciously or consciously, he rejoices that such handy weapons have been forged for him.

In that extraordinarily well-informed but brutally ignorant volume, "Where Freedom Falters," the latest pronouncement of the tory mind on things American, almost word for word the author quotes the opinions of the American hokum-hunter. He speaks of Mr. Mencken as *facile princeps*. Mr. Mencken is *facile princeps* if the object is the one I have been talking about, and no more absurd and confusing book to the foreign mind, not in its careful compilation of words, but in its deductions, has, for example, ever been written than Mencken's on the American language, save it be the annual English edition of Americana. Saint Leo Strachey, a fair-minded foreign visitor, has said the final say on the latter when, in American Soundings, he pointed out the fact that any Englishman, if he cared to, or any Frenchman, for that matter, could annually collect an equal amount of absurd sayings and opinions on the part of the lowly and ignorant of England or France, or from the columns of the provincial British or Gallic press.

A few years ago it was the custom for some of the more advanced American hokum-hunters to add glossaries of American words to the English printings of their books, under the assumption that no English reader could possibly understand a language that had become a combination of Mohawk, negro, and subway-New York. Under the assumption, I say, but I should have said under the apparent assumption, for, as a matter of fact, the gesture was one of precise smart-aleckry. One might just as well have published glossaries for the American editions of Thomas Hardy, John Buchan, or Arnold Bennett. The gesture, however, had its effect. Punch is still able to print such precious bits of international information as this: Fair Young American to Englishman (overwhelmingly entertained): "Say, you sure are a dim bulb to-night, aren't you?" Judging from the background, the conversation takes place in one of the better houses of New York. The world to-day is filled with Europeans who actually believe that within the next century Englishmen and Americans will no longer be able to converse with each other.

Facile princeps, Mr. Mencken, and a bad job well done.

Count Keyserling, whom elsewhere I have spoken of as having written a singularly penetrating criticism of America, returning to this country after an absence of fifteen years, and long before he even touches once more American soil, writes a series of articles utterly at variance with his earlier predictions, and showing in every line the effect of this spreading miasma. We are materialistic, mechanistic, and soulless. He even makes the astonishing statement that love is unknown in America, and that, to the young American, it has become merely a biological process. Where did he hear all this?

But there is no need to multiply instances. To the voices of Upton Sinclair, and the typical hokum-hunter, who does not know better and cannot know better, as I hope speedily to point out, are added the voices of such critics as Van Wyck Brooks and Thomas Beer, who should know better. The latter writes: "To go collecting raw materials in American history is to learn that Americans are a set of humorless prigs, but the pursuit is necessary and wholesome." So Americans are, lots of them, and frequently. But is this unpleasant trait peculiarly American and universally and perpetually national?

For my sins my desk is at present littered with English, Canadian, and even Australian letters, and in those which attack America—many of them are completely friendly and fair—there is hardly a sentence which is not lifted bodily from some American editorial, novel, or review, unconscious as the writers are of their indebtedness.

Our chickens have come home to roost with a

vengeance. But they are not chickens, they are cockatrices.

I trust I have made utterly clear that I am not opposed to criticism, self or otherwise, indeed, that I am greatly in favor of it no matter how savage, if implicitly or actually one is given to understand that there is, of course, another side to the picture. You cannot help but demand this other side if you have, as I have, something of a critical mind. Instead of adding glossaries of words the meanings of which any intelligent Englishman or European who speaks English can readily grasp from the context, the American hokum-hunter would do much more service to the cause of international peace and understanding if he would write a few forewords somewhat like this:

"Please! Do not take this too seriously. This is satire and, like all satire, is only half truth. In its entirety there is no such place as Main Street, or whatever the name of the street is, and if you will use your head a little you will see that there could not be in its entirety such a place. There never will be so long as men and women are what they are. Nor is there in its entirety any such town as Zenith, or whatever the town is called. There is no town where there are not at the worst a few pleasant, gentle, and intelligent people, even if the last trait is the result of instinct, not training. You know that as well as I do.

"That is the first point. Pray bear it in mind.

"The second point is that this novel (substitute editorial, article, etc.) was written originally for native consumption, for those, that is, who are able to sift the truth from the exaggeration and who, being able to do this, are not so likely to forget that all satire to be effective must be drawn in bold, crude strokes. When you read it, being a foreigner, remember, if you are an Englishman, that Charles Dickens, to take one of dozens, satirized early Victorian England in much the same way, and, if you are a Frenchman, that Anatole France was equally satirical of modern France, yet no one imagines that Victorian England was utterly brutalized or that modern France is utterly absurd and inept.

"Once more use your head and your discrimination, even if it is difficult to use these balancing instruments in the case of a new, far distant community, whose sudden rise to power and wealth and whose frequent bad manners are undoubtedly annoying, and whose construction is such that every man and every circle, no matter how foolish, can become articulate and find access to publicity. This last, incidentally, is merely a question of method, but in judging America it is one of the most important things to remember. There are just as many fools and just as many black areas of ignorance with you as with us, but with you these things are still kept under, with us they are aired. Take your choice. It is our opinion, perhaps our delusion, that if you admit sunlight to a sore you are much more likely to cure it. Moreover, we can't prevent this access to publicity no matter what we think.

"In a democracy all classes are taken seriously, as they should be; in ancient countries of aristocratic traditions the Babbitt and the peasant, until recently, if noticed at all, have been laughed at and spoken of as 'quaint.'

"The third point is that this novel (substitute editorial, article, etc.) being written by a hokum-hunter is, laying aside the already discerned one-half untruth of satire, only about a quarter true, anyhow. Do not forget that the hokum-hunter is usually so insecure in his philosophy that the most famous of recent American satires contained a huge and charming joke on the author of which he himself is probably still unaware. There are not many books where the original intention to contrast the beauty, wit, and intelligence of the heroine with the dullness of her environment turns itself into an even sharper satire upon pseudo-culture than upon the stark ignorance of the country-side."

But the average American hokum-hunter could not write such forewords for the following very simple yet very subtle reason. In nine cases out of ten he is actually just as ignorant of America in

America's more subtle aspects as the most uninstructed alien. He is born ignorant, remains ignorant, and constantly fortifies his ignorance. Indeed, he is worse off than an alien, for at least a few of them admit they do not know, whereas the American hokum-hunter is convinced he does know. He is convinced that he is the only person who does know. Like an East Indian fakir he sits cross-legged constantly peering into the crystal ball of his own misconceptions. This curious and twisted attitude would not be possible, could not survive, save in a democracy, and is symptomatic of faults and virtues peculiarly democratic. Or rather, it is symptomatic, once again, of a fault arising from the misuse of a virtue.

The reason why nobody mistakes the satire of a Dickens, or an Anatole France, or a Bernard Shaw for the complete picture of a nation is because there is always, implicit in the minds of such writers, the recognition of at least a modicum of something superior to what they are describing. Only in a democracy is it possible for a mean-minded man to imagine mean-mindedness universal. And again I say this is the abuse of a virtue because it is made possible by the amiable and indulgent attitude of even those democrats who know better. To understand this we must go back once more a little into history, and we must bear in mind the delicate, hidden processes of American life.

Literature is essentially aristocratic. And by that I mean aristocratic in the best sense of the term. If it is really literature it cannot be anything else. This has always been so, and will always be so. If writing fails in this respect, then, no matter what other virtues it may possess, it is merely ephemeral. The satire becomes a passing broadside, the romance a temporary street song. For writing, if it is to exhibit any permanency, must display, either actually or by implication, the leading principle of aristocracy which, rightly understood, is objectiveness. Perspective, that is; a trace of intelligent aloofness. A keen sympathy but an acute discrimination. Or, to put it in its simplest terms, a warm heart but a cool head. This has nothing to do with the birth, environment, or political or social beliefs of the writer. Neither has it to do with the subjects he or she chooses to treat. Neither am I referring to an objective or subjective method of telling a story. I speak simply and solely of this: the writer must be aware through his philosophy of something beyond and greater than himself, no matter what that thing may be. He may believe that man is born to blackness and dies without hope, but if he believes that, then he must also believe that man deserves a better fate. You see what I mean? No matter how hopeless a writer's point of view is he must have the impatience which can come only from the realization that there is real beauty, fineness, and greatness, no matter how little these things are realized. And how can you have that realization where humanity is concerned if you contemptuously believe that about you there is never any trace of beauty, fineness, or greatness? That you alone are born with those things in you? Not a chance. How can you have the objective point of view necessary to all important writing if you actually believe, for example, that a great nation of a hundred and twenty million human beings was founded on corruption and lives by hypocrisy?

Maxim Gorky is a communist, and has lived in the gutter, and, for the most part, writes of the gutter, but he writes, none the less, as an aristocrat; Lady Oxford writes of very grand people and events, but she does not write as an aristocrat—in the literary sense, I mean—nor does Upton Sinclair who also writes of fairly important people and events, if only to destroy them.

What irritates you in so much modern writing is not that it describes vulgar things, because nothing is too vulgar to be properly written about, but because a vulgar and pretentious mind is describing vulgar things, vulgarly unaware that there is such a thing as a lack of vulgarity.

Now, if we regard this question historically

where America is concerned we come across the following facts:

Within the last two decades thousands of young men who, thirty or fifty years ago, would have flung their imaginations into material development, where at the time they belonged, since the essence of poetry is not particularly to write verse but to lose yourself in the most imaginative episodes of your period, have been turned toward the professions, the government services, and the arts. We are overwhelmed with talent, half-baked. Material opportunity has enormously narrowed, a process which, with occasional breaks such as oil and motor-cars, and so on, is steadily increasing. To the ranks of these young men has been added a totally new force in the shape of young womanhood released. Furthermore, whatever else may be said of American education it has at least taught innumerable young people to read and write. Never, therefore, in the history of the world have there been so many critics and so many writers, potential or otherwise, as there are to-day with us. Never so many articulate people, or people desirous of being articulate. Never so many expressive people whose only expression is impatience. There is less end to the making of books than there was even in biblical or Shakespearian times. From what I can gather, fifty per cent of every class now graduating from our colleges and universities wants to write, and since writers, and other artists, and all people not actually in business, are by their natures and the permission of their circumstances, more or less inclined to rebellion and criticism, you have a vast new power constantly watching, analyzing, and changing the country. Indeed, you have the curious spectacle, as was the case to a lesser degree in the time of the muck-rakers, of numerous talented persons attacking the very institutions which, had these people been born twenty years or so earlier, they would have helped to found.

Since to express oneself legitimately seems to be the final happiness of life, all this new articulateness, save for the unavoidable noise, might be unqualifiedly a good thing were it not that in a democracy so many of the articulate fail to recognize any standards but their own—not only fail to recognize any standards but their own, but, as I have said, have no way of discovering others. At least, no way that will do them personally any good, although I believe that in the long run, democracy, being based on the trial and error method invariably kills evil off, leaving only what is good. In a generation or two, our brilliant uninstructed, although they themselves will be dead, will have followers whom time has instructed.

Meanwhile, we are suffering from too much

intelligence and too little common sense; too much opinion and too little knowledge; too much articulateness and too little discrimination. Too many people who because they are fools think every one else must be too. Any number of our hokum-hunters have all the gifts of the gods save the important ones of real knowledge and precise discernment, with the humility that these imply. It is therefore possible for them, when the fair-minded and, in consequence, hesitating foreigner asks, is this you have written actually true, to reply, not only true but not half true enough.

As I have said, the subtle and unique American social structure not only permits this but makes its rectification extremely slow. I have in mind, for example, an acquaintance who runs a literary column in New York. In every respect she is qualified for this important task save for the fact that she knows nothing of American life, can know nothing of American life, being of the type I have been describing, and, being an American, is not likely to have any one tell her. She is secure in her own shrinking self-conceit. But even if some one does tell her there is no obvious reason for her to believe what she is being told. It is an impasse; also it is a total misunderstanding of democracy. Critical and literary New York is filled with such shining, truncated talents. Thus every week the column in question goes out to spread nonsense about America all over the world and assure the hostile critics of America that their preconceptions are correct.

The American in certain ways is easy-going and too polite. This is due partly to his nature, partly to his living in a democracy. He is forced to be polite. The same conditions are observable in France. In a democracy one of the signs of good breeding is to temper opinion with courtesy, also, one of the requirements of safety is to use tact. The average hokum-hunter because of this has an advantage. It is entirely possible for a talented young man or woman to graduate from a university, meet all manner of people, live out his or her allotted span of years, and die quite untouched by scores of nuances of which other Americans are aware. This is particularly likely to happen if the talented young man or woman becomes a writer, an actor, a motion-picture success, or something of the kind.

In the American character there is still a childlike humbleness in the presence of what, rather absurdly, since it is exhibited in all human pursuits, is called "creative ability." Most of us have seen first-rate bank presidents put up with considerable impertinence from second-rate actors. I have an author friend, an extremely brilliant one, a very famous hokum-hunter, who, whenever he goes to a party, large or small, usually goes drunk. He not only goes drunk, he becomes noisy. As he begins to shout the minute he crosses the threshold and continues to shout until he leaves, the alcoholic mist which surrounds him is never dissipated. Because of this his knowledge of gentle manners in America is limited and he believes gentle manners do not exist, although he knows innumerable well-bred people, is frequently meeting others, and is constantly—but as a rule never more than once where any one family is concerned—going to well-bred houses. He knows there are well-bred people in England and France, because if he behaves with the same abandon in those parts of the world he is spoken to in no uncertain tones.

Americans have an odd, and to me it seems, unfortunate method of concealing their embarrassment at the antics of a guest, a method due partly, I suppose, to misty traditions of hospitality on the frontier, where you either shot a man or else put up with him. They try to pretend that nothing is going on at all except when, nervously, they laugh. This explains why numerous ill-bred foreign visitors leave with the impression that there is, in America, no such thing as breeding.

But there is no necessity to take such crudely dramatic examples. Any fairly talented, completely assured American can enter most American houses—at least once—and come away with the impression that the egregious nonsense he or she has talked or acted is subscribed to by the majority who have seen or listened. The motion-picture queen with the manners of a mad potentate remains totally unaware of how funny she is. Think what happens when this process is transferred to print where, for a week or two anyway, no one can answer, and then only from a distance. By imagining this you will understand better a good deal of American fiction and criticism. Yet, as I have said, domestically all this is not so important. Quarrels and bad manners within a household are often merely a sign of vigor and clear the air. It is only when the neighbors overhear, minus explanation, that falsehood and misinterpretation spread.

There is room for a very important new school of American writing, a school which will tell this country and the world, wisely, humbly, but firmly, what America really is. That satire will have its place in this telling, goes without saying. There is no great writing without satire, but in great writing, satire is human and sees beauty. It is the satire of a Thomas Hardy, an Anatole France, a James Cabell, not the satire of a Benjamin de Casseres. It is the blow of a giant, not the sting of a wasp. Where the world in general is concerned, however, I am afraid it is too late. The gross caricature of America by Americans has gone forth. I doubt if we can talk it down, we will have to live it down.

IX

THE FAILURE OF DEMOCRACY

****

IX

THE FAILURE OF DEMOCRACY

TWO or three months ago, Will Durant, author of "The Story of Philosophy," American, and Bertrand Russell, philosopher in himself and a fine one, Englishman, held a debate in which Durant maintained that democracy had failed and Russell maintained that it had succeeded. It had failed, Durant maintained because, as proven in the United States, it was a system which permitted government to fall entirely into the hands of professional politicians; it had succeeded, Russell insisted, because, as provcn by the United States, it had liberated the ordinary man and allowed him to prosper in a way no other political or social system had been able to accomplish.

Both were right in their premises; Russell alone was right in his deductions. Which shows the difference between a man who collects philosophy and one who thinks it. Only the actual philosopher can understand government.

But right or wrong, the debate was symptomatic of a fact all thinking Americans should recognize and consider in a way they have not yet done. It is no longer possible to be merely vaguely a democrat, democracy is once more, and more perilously than ever in its history, on trial before the world. Indeed, only on the American continents, North and South, is it any longer generally believed in, and even on those two continents the ranks of those who have ceased to believe are growing. Heretofore democracy has been on what might be called the up-grade and has been granted the sympathetic indulgence of all men of liberal tendencies. But that time has passed. Numerous political observers now feel, although wrongly, that democracy can be judged as a mature product, and as we all know, more is expected of maturity, less allowances are made for it. Just as with the party in power, democracy triumphant is in a more difficult position than democracy struggling. The party out of power can make promises; the party in power is expected to keep them.

Moreover, newer political experiments have arisen to challenge democracy, while, by a turn of the wheel, older and supposedly discredited political experiments seem new once more. In England, the Liberal Party, at the beginning of the war securely in power, is now the third in influence. To find on the map of Europe an actual democracy, that is, a democracy politically, socially, and spiritually democratic, requires a powerful field-glass. As a result, and certainly never more formidably, the inhabitants of the United States are called upon to prove the faith the majority live by. Not by argument alone, and certainly not by boastfulness and meaningless statement, but by cogent proof and appropriate action. Did he but know it, every citizen of the United States has become a walking symbol of democracy both in his private actions and in the way in which he permits his government, local or national, to function. In his goings up and down, here, there, and the other place, the eyes of the world in this respect are on him and by him democracy is being judged.

It is a position of trust, isn't it?

An English journalist, Alexander Mackay, publishing in 1849 a sympathetic description of the United States, assigns the boastfulness of that period to the fact that every American believed himself involved in the success of democracy and was eager to show himself the champion of democratic institutions. In our pride and power and present material ease, such championship may seem unnecessary, yet it is needed now—minus boastfulness; above all, minus boastfulness!—even more than in 1849.

Because of its position the United States must walk firmly, but, still more because of its position, it must walk softly and uprightly, for, as most people seem to fail to recognize, once you become the leading proponent of a marked political and social system you become the focus of hatred of all those forces throughout the world who see in that system the destruction of their own ideas. Life has never yet been a question of minding your own business and going about it. Half of it, the tragic half of it, invariably consists in preventing others from minding your business for you. Nor, and especially nowadays, can a great nation mind its own business exclusively, anyway. International interests are too interlocked for friction to be absent save when the most delicate common sense is used.

To the tory mind,—and, outside of America, it is a most powerful mind, recently rejuvenated and now controlling most European governments, —the United States stands for the horrors of democracy, just as Russia, to the democratic mind, stands for the horrors of communism, just as Italy, to the liberal mind, stands for the horrors of autocracy.

These are no theoretical horrors. They are not even merely political horrors. To the tory mind democracy means the uprooting of every ideal from how your tenant-farmer conducts himself to the manners and morals of your daughter. So long as democracy was weak, its dangers could be overlooked, but when democracy is strong its influence must be combatted. When hatred and fear of this kind reach a certain point of cohesion there is but one outcome in the present uncivilized state of mankind.

Indeed, the state of the world to-day could well be compared to that of 1815 when the tory reaction of the Holy Alliance was seeking by every means to extirpate the republicanism of Napoleon; a republicanism which, although it had ceased to be a political fact, was still a social fact since it allowed the common man to rise. But the tories of those days overlooked, and the tories of to-day overlook, one fact. Democracy as a reality not a theory has been steadily advancing. Science and invention, a multitude of other influences, have taken care of that. The ordinary man, for all the slave that he still may be, has been liberated, and you will never get him back where he started. The democrat may be wrong in many details of his present methods and the results may be disorderly and regrettable; the tory may be able temporarily to produce what seems—but only from the top looking down—an almost perfect state of affairs, yet philosophically and historically the democrat would seem to be right. He, at least, is riding the flood, however leaky his skiff may be, while the tory is attempting to hold it back.

Now, politically and socially, or in other words philosophically, there are just two types of mind with all their subdivisions—the democratic mind, and the tory mind. Back of almost every excuse now being given for the present dislike of the United States is this essential fact of the tory mind. When the European complains of "Americanization," he is not complaining of "Americanization," he is complaining of democracy, although he does not know it. When the European liberal meets this charge by saying that he is not complaining of democracy but the fact that the United States has fallen away from the democratic doctrines, in other words, that he is complaining not of theory but of practice, it is because, influenced by the wave of toryism, now sweeping Europe, he has lost sight of the enormous slowness of democracy; its huge arc; the fact that frequent and gross mistakes are inherent in the democratic system.

At all events, as Bertrand Russell pointed out, you must not compare a system of government with some remote ideal if you are making a practical judgment upon it. You must judge it, as you would a man, humanly. The ideal, for example, may be Christianity, but if you are just, also logical, you will compare a man not with this remote idea but with his fellows.

If democracy is no worse than any other form of government, then it is not a failure, and those who wish for it, even if it is more of a belief than a fact, have a right to it. But if, in adding up the peculiar vices and virtues of a democracy and comparing them with the peculiar vices and virtues of other forms of government, you find that democracy does indisputably promote certain benefits while by no means indisputably injuring certain other benefits, then democracy has not only not been a failure, it has had a modicum of success.

Still further, and most important of all, if, in tracing the history of a democracy, you find that one after another what were thought to be the peculiar vices of democracy have been cured or bettered, then democracy has not only had a modicum of success, but its future is hopeful, nor are its new vices any more likely to be permanent than its old.

Does democracy in the United States meet these tests? I think it does.

As an instance, we are as a nation far less imperialistic than we were twenty years ago. This, on the face of it, may not seem true, because American business, due to expansion, is just at present more imperialistic than it has ever been.

But politically and in the temper of the people, the United States has never been less imperialistic. As a result, and this has been shown dramatically two or three times within the past five years, as soon as the people realize clearly the imperialism of business they, most of them business men themselves, will curb and cure that imperialism.

Democracy is very much misunderstood. It is misunderstood even by the democratic mind save when that mind pauses to think clearly and carefully. Many times as democracy has been defined, it cannot be defined too much. To the present-day American nothing is more important than this redefinition, whether he makes it to himself or states it publicly.

Democracy is a political system, it is also a social system, but more than either it is a philosophical system; a religion, if you wish to call it that. In its practice it is a philosophy put into operation. To the right, it takes itself out in an individual's belief in a certain political system which will allow the philosophy to work; to the left, it takes itself out in the individual's point of view towards humanity. To the contrary, any tory system is largely pragmatic. Fundamentally, it is not a philosophy, merely a question of whether a thing works. Therefore, to a democrat his faith is as necessary as his works. A political system can go astray, a social system can be damaged, but if the philosophy is still there those who hold it believe that sooner or later both can be remedied. This is why, although the continued assertion of the American of his belief in democracy seems to the European, in the face of actuality, banal, sentimental, and frequently hypocritical, to the American it seems a matter of life and death. If he loses his philosophy, little as he may understand it, little as he may live up to it, little as he may even realize that it is a philosophy, he knows that democracy is done for.

The speeches of our statesmen, and more honest politicians, are not the tiresome repetitions of lip-service that Europeans or some of our own critics think them. They are the necessary ritual of the democratic faith and the assurances to the public that, however bad things may be, that faith is not entirely forgotten.

Rituals have their dangers. Obviously. But, except for the very brilliant and strong, the world cannot get on without them. Moreover, at their worst, they are assertions on the part of those making them by which the rest of mankind, should it wish, can check them up. Only the tory, and then only when he is in complete control, can remain silent and contemptuously refuse to explain his motives. Direct action is the prerogative of the autocrat alone.

Democracy is not only a philosophy, but it is a

philosophy based on evolution. Indeed, it is no more than evolution translated into political and social terms. Evolution is slow. So is democracy. Evolution works by the trial and error method. Evolution, therefore, is wasteful. So is democracy. But, when all is said and done, evolution is the only process which has yet produced a man.

The trial and error method means merely that you learn from mistakes, or successes, and not from what is told you. It is merely another name for knowledge acquired at first hand, and it has this great advantage. Much as it walks backward and forward, much as it stumbles, much as at times it even shelters reaction, permitting a democracy to appear for a while an autocracy, what eventually is learned is the secret of a common national experience, and national or racial experiences become part of the fibre of a race, of a nation. They are automatic and inevitable. It is not necessary to think about them. Much time as they have wasted in the beginning, they no longer waste time at all. The human race took centuries learning to walk erect, now walking erect is the least thing the normal man has to worry about.

For example, the United States is one of the few countries to-day where political or sectional rebellions do not represent possible future events. Sectional rebellion has been tried and the advantages of union have been proven. But in the beginning our sectional rebellion would not have occurred had it not been for the weakness inherent in democracy; a weakness that means subsequent strength. Nor is political rebellion any more likely. Nor is social revolution.

Political rebellion is not likely because every American knows that if events reach a crisis a new party will be formed, and that if the abuses have been too great this party will win. Either that, or else one of the older parties will be forced to change utterly its tactics. This has so often happened in the past, and there is so little to prevent it from happening in the present, that arguments to the contrary seem absurd. That such a process is slow, wasteful, sometimes tragic, is clear, and so the citizens of a democratic country hesitate to make the experiment, but once they do, the lesson they have learned is never forgotten.

For the same reasons, social revolution to the American of all classes is but the vaguest of considerations. Throughout the United States there are constantly going on a series of small and bloodless (sometimes, unfortunately, bloody) revolutions, and when these reach a certain degree of importance the nation as a whole takes cognizance of them, and their causes, at least partially, are cured. There is no need of any further argument in this direction except to point to the present position of the American laboring man. That many abuses are left, is true. That these perpetual small revolutions are wasteful; certainly. But their sum total is not half so wasteful as that of a French or Russian revolution.

Descending from graver matters to everyday ones and, therefore, to some minds possibly vulgar ones, there was a time when the American, save for the most refined, was famous for his spitting. He has ceased spitting, he will never spit again. Through disgust with his own habits, although, of course, helped by the cigarette, he has learned to amend them. But should something happen to the rulers of tory countries, the world will see for a while an expectoration, or its equivalent, that will make the earlier American essay appear the gentle amateur event it was. Spitting holds out numerous prospects of fun if you have never been allowed to spit. It is only by trying it yourself that you learn how selfish, disgusting, and unsanitary it is.

A suppressed class in any country is dangerous in direct proportion to the amount of repression and the size of the class.

To-day in the United States if you wish to find bad manners, gross materialism, and all the errors that are supposed wrongly by the tory mind to adhere to democracy, seek out the most newly arrived immigrant just escaped from the supposed good manners of toryism, or if you wish to find an utter lack of any desire for beauty, seek out an immigrant recently arrived from one of the more artistic countries of Europe. The American of older stock is no longer colt-like. For the most part he has gone through his period of bad manners. Having done the worst he could by his landscape, for example, he is now trying to improve it. I may be mistaken, but so far as I know the United States and Canada are the only modern countries which are setting aside great tracts of land for recreation only, where cities everywhere are deliberately setting out to make themselves beautiful, where there are growing movements to beautify gasoline stations and prohibit road signs. The American landscape is an excellent concrete example of democracy in action. Few will deny that it has been hideously defaced. But wait a few hundred years, and meanwhile regard those spots where this movement to beautify it has already been given impetus.

Democracy, being evolution, to be understood even in the slightest must be observed with the patience of the geologist or biologist; with the vision which regards not decades, or even centuries, but tens of centuries. The United States, one hundred and fifty years old, is by its very nature still an infant. Perhaps a thousand years from now, and that allowing for the speed of modernity and the United States in particular, the historian may be able to evaluate approximately the American experiment. Until then, he can only hope to separate out from the tangled skein of the present a few threads and, following them through from the beginning, speculate as to their future.

The tory country can be judged more swiftly and ruthlessly. There is no such impediment to continuous and speedy action as in a democracy. A man can run down-hill, and more prettily, than he can run up-hill. Against toryism history is the most damaging witness. The tory mind is the fundamentalist mind. It believes in a perfect creation produced by a wave of the hand and preserved by inexorable laws. In its phrase book there is no such sentence as circumstances alter cases; no such words as mutability or flexibility.

But to believe in evolution, at all events where it is applied to human affairs, it is necessary also to believe in something else, without which this sort of evolution falls to pieces. You must believe in the urge toward superiority, conscious or unconscious, on the part of the average man and woman.

With my democratic bias I cannot see how any open-minded student of history can deny this urge.

That as it first emerges it is likely to take itself out in ugly and uncomfortable ways is no doubt true, and a democracy bears witness to this fact, but as the instinct becomes trained, either in the individuals where it first appears or in the generations which follow, the ugly and uncomfortable features tend to disappear. In other words, it seems to me that a democracy, since it is evolution, since it is in microcosm the history of the human race, must run the gamut of almost every form of absurdity, childishness and wastefulness, before, in the end, it produces a universal and inherent beauty, order, and intelligence never before achieved by any political system. Nor does the fact that each generation biologically and socially is inclined to repeat the ancient errors invalidate this statement. These errors are mostly what are known as moral errors, personal errors, the root of which, the nature of which, have never been accurately charted or understood. Politically, and socially in a large way, the human race does not repeat its errors in their entirety when anything approaching an opportunity for universal experience is given. It does slowly progress. It does not progress, however, when there is class rule, for then only the ruling classes can enjoy these experiences, and other classes, in order to share, must upset the ruling class by revolution. After which, we have for a while merely a completely wasteful turning over; a repetition without any progress.

For instance, the communistic government of Russia, which is rapidly ceasing to be communistic, will have accomplished just what? If it is lucky, eventually, and after infinite blood and misery, it will accomplish just what the democracy of the United States has already accomplished. It will have liberated the ordinary man and have given him opportunity. It will not have destroyed class; it will not have destroyed inequality of wealth. In order to accomplish what democracy has accomplished, it will merely have substituted one class for another and in so doing have destroyed whatever good, the result of slow centuries, there may have been in the class that has been annihilated.

That this urge toward superiority, given free rein as it has been given in the United States, has been at work, and that even in the short space of one hundred and fifty years the upward trend can be clearly distinguished, seems to me evident. You can select any one of a dozen threads from the tangled skein.

Let us take Will Durant's charge that democracy has failed, because democratic government inevitably falls into the hands of professional politicians and thus no longer is a government by the people and for the people.

To begin with, certain terms, carelessly used, must be investigated. Democratic government does fall into the hands of professional politicians, indeed, it falls into their hands almost the moment it starts. But then, so does every other form of government, and so will every form of government conceivable to the human mind. If any one can pick out in history any government to which this does not apply, he will be rewriting history. He will not only be rewriting it, he will be making it up. The difference between, let us say, Louis the XIVth and the late Mr. Croker was merely one of title and the not unimportant fact that Mr. Croker could be impeached and Louis the XIVth couldn't. If those famous professional politicians Metternich, Bismarck, Machiavelli, and Richelieu are typical of tory government, and at least their names have survived when others have been forgotten, democracy has nothing especially to fear in comparison.

The gravest charge that can be brought against the American mind is its lack of historical perspective. In its charges against its own country, it frequently displays the most extraordinary lack of knowledge of what has gone before. One would be led to believe that political graft was an American invention; that political ruthlessness was invented by General Jackson's "gang." It would not even be surprising to find some American critic stating that Benedict Arnold discovered treason.

In direct proportion to the size of a country and the complexity of its problem does its government fall into the hands of professional politicians. The same is true of a city or a town. How could it be otherwise? Politics is a business, and an intricate one. If every man spent all his time, even the major portion of it, governing his country, little else would be accomplished. If I am not mistaken, the failure of the Greek democracies was due to the number of amateur politicians, idle because of slave labor. Personally I have never been able to understand the ignominy implied in the term professional politician. You might as well sneer and say, professional plumber, professional dentist, professional architect.

The same applies to the ignorant use of the words, political machine. What is the difference between a political machine and any other organization formed for the purpose of conducting business? If you deny the political machine, then you deny the need business has for organization.

These delusions arise from the remnants of an ancient tory idea that government is the task of a certain rich class, relieved by their wealth from any temptation toward financial dishonesty but by no means relieved, as history shows, from the temptations of the lust of power, of place, and of class cruelty. That Will Durant, in common with many Americans, shares in these delusions is evident from his further statement that, although democracy in the United States has fallen into the hands of professional politicians and is no longer a government by the people and for the people, none the less he could largely forgive it if it were a government of the best people?

What does he mean by the best people? Unconsciously he is harking back to the ancient tory idea I have mentioned. Class rule is a dangerous thing as the records of various nations have shown. It may be excellent for the class in power, but it is fatal for the rest of the country. And who knows, anyway, what the best people are, and who is fit to choose them? The best people, once entrenched in power, have a singular habit of turning into the worst people. As a practical instance, I have never been able to see the difference between a United States Senator who buys his seat—and very few of them do—and a British peer who buys his peerage, save that the former invariably regrets his action and the latter does not. Save, also, for the extremely essential and saving democratic fact that the buying of seats in the United States Senate becomes at once such a public scandal that it is not likely to grow into a habit. It remains, in other words, sporadic.

The point is not whether the government of a

country falls into the hands of professional politicians and political machines, for that the government of any country is bound to do, the only question is whether these machines and politicians sufficiently register public opinion, as Will Durant claims in the United States they do not; whether they have been doing this progressively, with, of course, inevitable set-backs, since the country began; and whether the personnel of these machines has been steadily degenerating and no longer represents an accurate cross-section of the country.

As far as I can make out in not one of these respects has democracy in the United States failed, and in not one of these respects has there been a lack of progress, despite numerous backslidings and numerous eras of fairly black shame. Mr. Durant must not be misled by the scorn of the average man, especially the intelligent one, for politics. In every country, and in every age, the average citizen has complained and has scorned the politician, but only in a democracy, save by means of a revolution, has this scorn a chance of becoming effective.

England is supposed to have a very high type of government and yet the Public Orator of Oxford University, Mr. Poynton, speaking recently, and in the character of a pupil of Socrates, said: "You English people make a sorry bungle of anything connected with the state, but your voluntary achievements are wonderful; your Boy Scouts, your Girl Guides, for instance." Lord Bryce, a good many years ago, said the same thing about the United States. He maintained that democratic government would become more and more a question of professional politicians running the business of the government, with voluntary organizations effecting the really important and necessary changes. We have seen, of course, that such voluntary organizations, in the shape of lobbies, can be extremely dangerous as well as useful, but they too are subject to the democratic process of betterment and experience.

As a matter of fact, the electorate of the United States now works as a gigantic voluntary organization; a gigantic lobby that ever so often expresses its will, prescribes the general policy, and then goes back to its proper place. And that is just as it should work, so long as it remains watchful. That it does remain watchful is proven by the fact that when it wants so to do it directly reverses the general policy. I suppose no one will deny that the defeat of President Wilson expressed exactly the will of the majority of the people at that time. When the party now in power ceases to express the will of the majority of the people, it will no longer remain in power. And this will of the majority has never been so evident as at present. There has never been a time in the history of the United States when every interest has been so represented, not only in the actions of the government, but in the personnel of that government.

That there are abuses, injustices, absurdities, is obvious; that to cure these under the democratic system is a laborious and slow process is also obvious; but that nothing but a democratic government would allow these abuses, injustices, and absurdities even to come to the surface is also obvious, let alone attempting to cure them.

As to the personnel of our present generation of professional politicians, as to the workings of the average political machine, those are delicate and hotly debatable questions, but I, for one, am convinced that in these respects, as in most others, there has been a steady improvement. We are accustomed to compare present achievement with the achievement of the founders of the country. That is not fair. The country is a far more complex organization than it was in 1800: the founders of any country are usually the very highest type of men; the country seldom remains for any length of time the near-Utopia it was when first conceived. In order to discern whether the United States has progressed or degenerated, politically, socially, and intellectually, the critic should start in about 1830.

If he will study conditions from then on, he will not, I think, remain depressed.

If any one will state that the political and diplomatic mind, save amongst the leaders of a country, is not likely to be the highest type of mind, I will be inclined to agree with him, but, taking that into consideration, and even taking into consideration the direct election of Senators, I would like to have proven to me, by facts, not statements, that the Government of the United States, by and large, in all its departments is not a more dignified proceeding than it has ever been in its history, save, perhaps, for those bright years between 1776 and 1829. And even those years were not so bright as many people think them. I find that most people who deride, let us say, the personnel of the Senate, when they are questioned exhibit entire ignorance of that personnel. This is a test I have tried many times. Starting as an arbitrary example, with Cutting, of New Mexico, and working through to Moses, of New Hampshire, this personnel, although it may often be mistaken, compares well in dignity with any other upper-house in the world. When undignified people are elected to this body they are speedily laughed into silence or out of office. Indeed, sometimes these undignified people are unconscious agents of good. Many a backward state has been awakened by an undignified Senator.

Once more, one of the benefits of a democracy is that a fool in a high place is more easily isolated and more easily retired than a fool under a tory system of government. There is no delusion that a fool, simply because he is a gentleman, is any less of a fool.

I find that the same people who writhe uneasily because of the personnel of our representative bodies, about which they know nothing, are equally ignorant of the personnel and accomplishments of our government bureaus, of their intelligence, honesty, and record of hard work; of the experts who man them; of the vast improvement over the bureaus of previous years. These servants of the government are not always honest. No, of course not. They are not always intelligent. During the stress of great wars instances of stupidity and dishonesty are likely to come to the surface, but if you know anything about these bureaus at all, you will know that evolution has been effectively leavening them. For one thing, the spoils system, formerly their basis, has been replaced by a real fervor for accomplishment and governmental service.

As political machines become smaller they are likely to become more corrupt, less dignified, for the rewards do not attract as high a type of man. The political machine that governs a city is not as likely to be as honest or intelligent as the machine that governs a country, but even here, it seems to me, the impartial observer can find an improvement in American affairs, both in personnel and accomplishment. The Tammany of to-day is nothing like the Tammany of forty years ago; in even the most corrupt city—and there are far too many of them—the political rings are required to give a return for the money they steal that would have outraged the ward politicians of half a century ago. The present shame of Indiana is an encouraging sign, not a discouraging one. Fifty years ago there would have been so many companions in shame that Indiana would not be occupying the prominent place it does to-day.

To my way of thinking, you can take any other skein of American life and, following it through, arrive at the same conclusion. The skein of increasing honesty and intelligence in business; the skein of a more worldly and less provincial point of view; the skein of an increasing interest in the things of the mind; the skein of maturity and wisdom; the skein of the comfort of living as opposed to mere luxury without comfort. A dozen other skeins. And so long as this evolutionary process is discernible I am not overwhelmed by any temporary thunder storms.

If numerous people wish to run up and down the country in nightshirts committing outrages, although any possible victim should be protected and all outrages severely punished, the paraders should be allowed to parade until they drop from exhaustion. If you have a fractious horse you exercise him, you do not keep him in the stable. Mr. Durant's supposition and the supposition of the tory mind—for the socialistic mind and the tory mind are alike in their belief in direct action and their real contempt for the ordinary citizen; their denial of any urge toward superiority—is that if enough people parade in their nightshirts, pretty soon every one will be parading in his nightshirt and the country will become a nightshirt land. To the contrary, the democratic belief is that in every country there are born too many strong people who have an instinctive dislike for nightshirts, save in their proper places, to permit this to happen, and that an over-use of the nightshirt eventually strengthens the hands of these people, just as it weakens the ranks of the paraders.

I am not even depressed by our record of crime or our conduct of murder trials, perhaps at present the principal charges being brought by the tory mind to prove the failure of democracy. Indeed, from a large point of view, I find both encouraging and arguments in favor of democracy, not against it. There are new factors at work that will eventually force for the first time in history a real appreciation of crime and possibly a real cure for it. Crime has always been with the world. Because of the growing misery and humiliation of our position in this respect, before long we will find ourselves taking drastic steps, and these drastic steps will of necessity be intelligent ones. To suppose that any great and peaceful community will allow itself to be conquered, or even continually insulted by crime is absurd. Yet, on the other hand, mankind will not move until it has to. It is only when conditions become impossible that they are changed.

Crime is no more inevitable than yellow fever. When, for the first time in history, a great nation is forced to investigate the causes of crime, as shortly we will be forced to do, as our engineers were forced to investigate the causes of yellow fever in building the Panama Canal, then crime will be cured because the conditions that make it will be cured. The plagues that swept Europe in the Middle Ages were the mothers of sanitation and preventative medicine.

Furthermore, crime is usually no more than energy and a certain amount of imagination misused and misplaced. It might be called energy minus character. The lack of crime in countries where there are vast suppressed populations, where suppression is part of the average man's point of view, does not seem to me a subject for particular congratulation. To begin with, under such circumstances, no attempt will ever be made, effectively, to cure crime; to end with, lack of energy in itself is no virtue.

For the same reason our criminal justice, dreadful as it may be as a present spectacle, is not philosophically a hopeless one. The American's dislike for inflicting capital punishment, a dislike that has been present all through his history, is not a sign of sentimentality or barbarism, it is a sign of civilization and logic. Nor is it contradicted by the American's predilection for personal violence. Both are part of a whole. The injured citizen realizes the hesitation his fellow citizens will experience in punishing, under the present laws, the man who has injured him. This present article is no argument for or against capital punishment, but every intelligent man knows that our present procedure, far from diminishing crime, promotes it, and this same intelligent man is gradually coming to the conclusion that it is the dignity, sureness, and inevitable swiftness of punishment that is the deterrent, not its severity. It is this dignity, sureness, and formidable celerity that frightens the criminal. The criminal has not the constructive imagination to visualize the actual punishment. If he had he would not be a criminal. At all events, there is an impediment in our major justice and this impediment must be removed. As far as I am personally concerned, the object would seem to be to get murder out of the world, not to perpetuate it by reserving to any government the right legally to perform it.

It is perhaps in the essential idea of democracy itself that the evolutionary urge toward superiority can be as clearly traced in the American mind as anywhere else. The most difficult charge to answer of all those made against democracy, and one frequently made even by the friends of democracy, is that although democracy may liberate and enrich the mass of the population, it has a constant tendency to pull down to one common level the extraordinary man. Matthew Arnold said that unless an American thought like his fellows he had to emigrate. To-day I should say that one of the surest ways to become famous and prosperous, and with increasing emphasis, is not to think like your fellows. But however that may be, if you will trace from 1776 to the present the American's idea of equality you will notice curious changes.

No critic who knows anything of American history believes for one moment that the words "all men are created equal" meant to the men who stated this philosophical proposition more than the ideal that all men should have, as much as humanly possible, equal opportunity. But the words have been distorted both by the unthinking democrat and the hostile tory.

This country started as a small aristocratic republic. In 1829 it became for a while the home of a mistaken idea of democracy. Whatever may have been the other virtues fermenting in the mass, there is no doubt that to the average American, for many decades, equality meant not so much the opportunity to become, through hard work and training, the equal of the best, but the opportunity to claim that, no matter how ignorant or inefficient you were, you were the equal of the best, anyway. It is on this rock that many democracies have foundered in the past. The amateur spirit properly understood is often a magnificent thing, but the amateur spirit misunderstood is the source of bad manners, stupidity, and poor service. For every American to believe that he can become president is an excellent idea, but for every American to believe that no further effort is needed is a wretched and dangerous idea.

That this latter belief has largely disappeared from the American mind is evident on every side; not only in the improved quality of American life, its manners and point of view, but in the improved quality of American work and craftsmanship. The growing complexity of existence, science among other factors, has informed the American that in order to succeed, knowledge, politeness, and intelligence are required. He has also been informed how to appreciate and reward talent in every direction. The gate of opportunity is still wide open, but it is more closely guarded, and you have to prepare yourself better in order to pass through it. Surely this is no charge against democracy. Democracy fails only when the gate is closed.

And the gate cannot be closed unless two misfortunes happen. The gate can only be closed when a democratic government becomes an aloof bureaucracy, or when the citizen who has succeeded, losing his democratic point of view, is no longer anxious to discover and reward talent. The former danger is inherent in every form of government and can only be avoided by vigilance; the second cannot happen until the whole fabric of American life and the basis of the American philosophy undergo changes which do not seem likely.

Many years ago Bernard Shaw, writing to Count Tolstoy on the nature of the Deity, spoke as follows, and if you substitute for the name of the Deity the word democracy, you have a perfect description of what I have been trying to say. "To me," Shaw wrote, "God does not as yet exist, but there is a creative force constantly struggling to evolve an executive organ of Godlike knowledge and power; that is, to achieve omnipotence and omniscience, and every man and woman born is a fresh attempt to achieve this object."

THE END